Army
Chaplain
Field Manual

Army Chaplain Field Manual

SOLDIER MENTAL HEALTH

P. Forrest Talley, Ph.D.

TETON PRESS

Army Chaplain Field Manual

To my children, Dominique, Gabriel, Clairissa, and Tessa.
Your genuine concern for others, guided by Christian sentiment,
and formed on the anvil of sober realism, inspires me.
My hope is that some of that practical, Christlike,
perspective comes through in the following pages.

A Note About Personal Pronouns

Throughout this book the personal pronouns 'he', 'him', 'his' will most often be used when referring to soldiers. Obviously this is not intended to dismiss the service or contributions of female soldiers.

These pronouns are employed because they make for less awkward sentence construction than using she/he, or mangling sentences that have a singular subject/object with the plural 'they.'

Moreover, nearly all readers will also recognize when these pronouns are used as synecdoches. That is, a literary device in which a part of something is substituted for the whole. If I were to write that 'We threw the pig skin around just for fun', everyone would understand that this included the lacing, rubber liner, threading *and* the pig skin. If you were to look at my car and exclaim 'Nice wheels', I would understand you were referring to the entire vehicle (I would also question your judgment).

CONTENTS

Appendices

ACKNOWLEDGMENTS

The motivation for writing this book came from my deployment to Iraq in 2008/2009. During my time in theater I had the great privilege of working with many soldiers and a number of chaplains. Three things became clear. One, there are a great many soldiers struggling with a variety of stressors, and very often these become significant mental health issues. This is not only a personal challenge for the solider, but a problem for the Army as it can degrade a soldier's ability to carry out his duties. Two, most soldiers trust chaplains a great deal more than they trust clinical social workers, psychiatrists and psychologists. Three, chaplains are more than capable of helping soldiers with a variety of mental health concerns. All that is required is some additional knowledge provided in a clear and systematic format. This volume was written guided by that objective.

With that in mind, I am grateful to all the soldiers (as well as the Marines, Airmen and Seamen) who trusted me to assist them during their deployment. I am also indebted to those chaplains that I had the pleasure of working with, and in so doing developed a better understanding of their role and the concern they have for their 'flock.'

The writing of this book began while I was attached to the USAR 2nd Medical Brigade. CPT Sullenberger, who was the commander at that time, graciously agreed to have me devote some of my drill time to writing this manual. Likewise, I want to thank COL Harris (who headed up the medical team) for his support in this endeavor. Not content to simply 'mark time' during drill weekends, he exemplified an aggressive and practical approach calling for reservists to do whatever they could to use their civilian skills to improve the lives of soldiers. I was pleased to serve under his command.

Dominique Inkrott, my oldest daughter, graciously took on the task of proof reading the manuscript, cleaning up grammatical blunders, double checking references, updating resources, and more. The field manual is significantly better for having been the object of her efforts and attention. I am extremely grateful. Whatever errors and oversights remain are entirely due to my own uncanny abilities, first identified by my ninth grade English teacher, to take a perfectly good sentence and visit linguistic harm upon its structure.

In addition, I must thank my wife and children who patiently dealt with their 52-year-old husband/father deciding to join the Army during a time of war, with a subsequent deployment, and later on with the numerous times I was absent while fulfilling my military obligations. To say I am thankful falls far short of expressing the gratitude I have for their support.

Lastly, I am likewise indebted to my father, a former chaplain in the Navy during WWII, a lifelong Baptist minister, and marriage and family therapist, whose life's work demonstrated how the role of chaplain and counselor can be effectively integrated.

SECTION I

INTRODUCTION

L ife in the military presents formidable challenges, many of them unique to the armed services. These include frequent moves, separation from family, loss of freedoms that civilians take for granted, deployments, and of course war-related stressors. In spite of these challenges, America's military men and women have a rich history of persevering, of staying true to their course, and completing their mission. Such dedication and sacrifice, however, is not without cost. To maintain a singular focus on accomplishing the mission, to place service to country above all else, putting family, friends, and personal desires behind this objective creates tremendous pressures on those who have stepped forward to shoulder this burden.

With this in mind, we should be clear that it is not a matter of whether a soldier will experience significant stress – it is an inevitable aspect of military service. No doubt the degree of stress will vary according to the soldier's MOS, duty station, deployments, command structure, mission, and other variables. Regardless of these differences, to some degree or another, the unique stressors of military service will impact every service member. Some will respond with exemplary resilience while others may prove unusually reactive to these pressures.

The difference in how one service member responds compared to another may be due to differences in their upbringing, genetics, the choices they make, the command under which they operate, or a variety of other factors. No matter the cause, however, when a soldier's response to stress is severe enough that his mission readiness is jeopardized, the chaplain's unique skill set and status place him in an ideal position to help.

It is commonly understood that the chaplain is the one who is typically first called upon for advice when an NCO, or officer, is worried about the mental health of a soldier under his command. Moreover, when soldiers are under great stress it is the chaplain that they confide in above all others. This may be due to the extra privacy protections that attach to the chaplain/soldier relationship, or it may be that the chaplain's position as a spiritual advisor imbues him with a distinctive sense of trust. Whatever the reason, chaplains are at the vanguard of the Army's efforts to assist distressed soldiers.

With this in mind, chaplains must acquire competency in recognizing mental disorders, and likewise have at least a basic understanding of how to effectively respond. Most chaplains understand that this comes with the job, that in essence, they are mental and spiritual medics.

The goal of this manual is to help chaplains meet this challenge. Having trained mental health interns and staff for over 20 years, and having been in the Army for nearly ten years, I am convinced that every chaplain is capable of mastering the material contained in this manual.

What This Field Manual Provides

This manual provides you with a concise summary of the most common presentations of mental health concerns you are likely to come across. Examples of these include generalized anxiety, major depression, post-traumatic stress disorder, traumatic brain injury, alcohol/drug abuse, and so forth.

By developing a working familiarity with these disorders and diagnoses you will be better able to develop effective solutions for distressed soldiers. Also, you will feel more confident when discussing a soldier's presentation with mental health professionals.

It is important to note, however, that no diagnostic nosology is big enough, or so richly elaborated, or finely nuanced, as to be a fully adequate framework from within which a chaplain can conceptualize all of his work. The efforts of chaplains takes place within the intersection of the physical, mental, and spiritual realms – the diagnostic constructions used within clinical psychology cannot adequately capture this richness.

Despite this shortcoming, the diagnostic categories we examine will prove helpful to the chaplain's work of assisting distressed soldiers. This is true in the same way that a two-dimensional map is helpful to the soldier during land navigation. Anyone who uses a map understands that its flat surface and topographical lines are far from the rich reality it is intended to portray. Nevertheless, in the hands of a skilled navigator, it becomes an exceptionally helpful tool for finding one's destination.

This does not, however, require that you become an expert diagnostician. Far from it. In fact, research shows that professionals often disagree when coming up with a specific diagnosis for any given individual (Al-Huthail, 2008). If a good deal of disagreement is the baseline among professionals who are diagnosing patients, there is certainly no pressure for chaplains to exceed this threshold.

Nor is there a practical need for you to become a Top Gun diagnostician. What will be helpful is for you to become adept at being able to make broad diagnostic conclusions. For example, to be able to distinguish between someone who is depressed versus someone who is psychotic. Or recognizing when a soldier is primarily dealing with simple anxiety versus PTSD.

Developing this level of skill is well within your reach, and made much easier by the structure of this manual which walks the reader through various diagnoses by clearly highlighting their distinctive features.

How The Manual Is Structured

In the first section of the manual, we examine five common mental health disorders. These include:

Generalized Anxiety Disorder
Post-Traumatic Stress Disorder (PTSD)
Depression
Thought Disorders
Adjustment Disorder

A separate chapter is devoted to each of these disorders. The format of each chapter follows a similar seven-part structure:

1. To provide a richer context, each chapter begins with a clinical vignette showing how the disorder presents in real life
2. A diagnostic description that focuses on the major symptoms
3. A brief description of how the disorder develops over time
4. Insights regarding how to assess for the disorder
5. Symptom Checklist Summary (a handy bullet point list of symptoms)
6. Descriptions of chaplain-oriented interventions
7. Intervention Checklist Summary (bullet point list of interventions)

The third section of the manual is devoted to examining sundry other issues. Some of these topics include disorders or problems that you may not frequently come across but are nevertheless important to recognize. This includes the following:

- Suicide Assessment
- Panic Attack Disorder
- Response to Sexual Assault

- Drug and Alcohol Abuse
- Traumatic Brain Injury (TBI)
- Personality Disorders

The field manual also contains an Appendix with important information. This includes a guide for how chaplains can best conduct an interview that yields the information needed to devise an effective course of action. Some brief questionnaires are also found in the Appendix, as is a guide for determining when you should refer to a mental health professional.

Also, the Appendix contains separate sections with summaries of each diagnosis. These summaries allow you to easily refer to a specific psychological concern and find the key symptoms and interventions for that disorder or problem. (It would be wise to make copies of these sections and have them readily available to refer to during interviews with troubled soldiers).

How To Best Use This Field Manual

Throughout this manual, you will find descriptions of common psychotherapeutic approaches used to treat a variety of mental health disorders. This is not done with the thought that you will be providing in-depth psychotherapy (although certain readers will certainly have the training and skills to do so, that is not an expectation). Instead, my intent is to help you become more familiar with the subject matter.

I want you to be thoroughly conversant with the topics discussed in each chapter. The better your understanding of each disorder and subject discussed in the manual, the better you will be able to intervene on a soldier's behalf. It may be that the soldier refuses to go to mental health, and the responsibility falls on you to develop an intervention plan. On the other hand, it may be that the soldier agrees to see a therapist, and you are called to effectively advocate for the soldier's well-being in this regard.

Either way, the greater your familiarity with each topic discussed in this manual, the greater your effectiveness. Chaplains are at the tip of the spear in helping to maintain both the spiritual and mental well-being of soldiers. Developing a basic proficiency with the information contained in this field manual will simply increase your effectiveness in pursuing that mission. If you have questions or recommendations you can reach me at info@forresttalley.com.

SECTION II

Common Mental Health Disorders

ANXIETY

S ergeant Copeland was one of those rare soldiers who never missed a chapel service – at least not when he was on the FOB rather than being on a mission. He was in his fifth month of a 15-month deployment as a driver in the 26th BSB (Brigade Support Battalion) in Iraq.

The sergeant was a quiet man. Reserved. Some would say aloof. Expressions of emotion were rare, and his overall demeanor was one of tense restraint. Like a guitar string tuned several keys too high.

Although respected for his skills and hard charging work ethic, none of his fellow soldiers had become close with him. Being a loner seemed a conscious preference. But his steadfast attendance at chapel made him standout in the mind of Chaplain Danek. Even more impressive was that the young sergeant studiously scribbled notes while listening to each sermon. On more than one Sunday Danek attempted to strike up a conversation with the young man. To say they were one-sided would be generous: the chaplain felt they were more similar to monologues.

With this in mind, it was understandable that Chaplain Danek was a bit perplexed when the young sergeant came to his office one morning and asked if he had a few minutes to spare. After pulling up a chair Copeland proceeded to study the floor. His expression was like that of the family dog who expects to be punished when his master comes home. Slowly exhaling he began to confide to the chaplain what was on his mind.

During the last couple of months the sergeant had found himself getting increasingly distracted, even while on missions where his focus had always been very sharp. This created pitched anxiety. In fact, Copeland was terrified by the thought. There was no room for error when you went outside the wire, and having his "head in the game" was essential if he were to keep his men safe.

The sergeant's sleep was suffering as well. No matter how tired he felt at the end of the day, as soon as he laid down on his rack his mind began to race. Unwanted thoughts crashed into his awareness, causing knots in his stomach and tension across his chest. Past conflicts he had with other soldiers frequently resurfaced and took on irrational importance. Questions about whether he should re-enlist when his contract was completed begged for immediate resolution. Most distressingly the unknown of whether he would survive the deployment painted morbid images in his imagination.

The worries would grow as he lay staring at the ceiling of his CHU. They would build like a wave rushing to shore, recede for a moment, and then rush back in crowding out all other thoughts. The sergeant would eventually feel trapped in a thick fog of racing thoughts.

At this point, he would jump out of bed, walk outside and sit on the stoop smoking. The rules on the FOB forbid this: he should have walked to the smoke pit, but he didn't care anymore. When smoking didn't work he would open a Red Bull and chug it down in one long draught. Nothing seemed to help except the eventual onset of insurmountable physical fatigue, and then the curtains of consciousness would slowly close, allowing the young soldier a brief but fitful sleep. Within a few hours, he was back awake with a long day of duties in front of him.

As Copeland spoke he continued to rub his hands against his thighs, frequently punctuating his remarks with " You know what I'm saying?" Although the sergeant tended to ramble, the chaplain was able to follow the thread of his thinking. As Copeland described the battle he had with worries, a few pointed questions showed that this tendency was not new. It could be traced back to his childhood when it presented in a much less intense form.

*"But this, what's happening now... it's different. Like a lot worse."
Copeland choked out the last words as though anguished to admit some
weakness.*

*"Sounds like a tough few weeks, Sergeant," Danek replied. "Have
you found anything that helps?"* The young man described having tried to
cope by working out more, smoking more, dipping more, and buying energy
drinks from the PX by the case.

*" Yeah, well, I'm not so sure that energy drinks will do much for your
stress levels," Danek chuckled.* In response, Sergeant Copeland shot a hard
look at the chaplain, clearly not finding any humor in his observation.
They continued to talk and Danek discovered that the sergeant was not
married and that he did not have strong ties to family or friends back in
the states.

He did, however, mention having several close friends in the military.
What's more, until the past couple of months he had gotten along very well
with other soldiers in his unit, but as his irritability increased so did the
tensions between him and other team members.

As they talked further Copeland admitted that he wasn't one to "spill
his guts" to a stranger, or "anyone else for that matter." Things had gotten
so bad, however, that he was now terrified that his lack of focus would get
someone killed on a mission. He knew he needed help, so swallowing his
pride he decided to speak with the chaplain.

"Do you think it might be time to consider redeploying back home?"
Danek asked, trying very hard to assume a matter of fact tone. He knew
that such a question could easily be seen as a negative judgment call about
a soldier's character.

*"I can't do that," Copeland responded adamantly. "I couldn't live
with myself if I didn't finish the deployment. I just can't do that."* The
chaplain was glad to hear that Copeland wasn't trying to win a ticket
home. Although rare, he had seen his share of soldiers trying to game the
system and find a way to punch an early return ticket stateside.

They continued to talk until the chaplain felt confident he had a good grasp of what was going on, and what might be done to provide this young soldier with some help.

"I'm glad you came to see me, Sergeant. I know it can be tough to talk about these things, but the good news is you don't have to keep struggling with this by yourself. From what you've told me it sounds like you've been anxious for many years, and this deployment has just made things worse. That makes sense; these deployments put stress on everyone. But I think there are some things we can do to take the edge off. Things that will help you relax a bit and stay focused on the mission."

Although he did not respond, SGT Copeland looked noticeably relieved. "It may surprise you, Sergeant, but you're not the only soldier that gets these feelings. Happens to a lot of us. But for you, it seems to stay at a pretty high level. What's more, I'm concerned that your lack of sleep is just making things worse - a lot worse. It's causing you to depend on nicotine and energy drinks to stay alert. The problem is that these things are also likely to make your anxiety worse. That, in turn, is making your sleep deteriorate, even more, in which case you probably feel like you need to smoke more, drink more coffee, energy drinks, etc. In the end, that's just a death spiral."

Danek had chosen his words carefully. He wanted to be sure to get Copeland's attention. "Death spiral" might do the trick. He hoped so because what he was about to suggest to the sergeant would be difficult.

"Damn. I don't want to die Chaplain."

Danek shook his head and elaborated. "Well, I don't know about you dying, but relying on cigarettes and energy drinks only makes things worse. I get it, I understand why you turned to those things, but to tell you the truth they are screwing up your mental state. Don't suppose I could get you to cut back?"

Copeland took a moment to consider the suggestion. "If I cut back on my dip or any of that sh-- sorry chaplain, I mean...if I cut back, I don't know if I can stay awake during the day." Danek let that response hang in the air, hoping the sergeant might reconsider.

24

When Copeland remained silent Danek decided to continue. "OK, I see your point. Maybe you would be willing to try some other approaches to getting your anxiety under control, and if we gain a little traction using those things maybe you would then be willing to think about cutting back on nicotine, coffee, and all of that stuff?"

"What do you have in mind?" Copeland asked.

"One thing I want to suggest is that you see someone over at Combat Stress Control--"

Before he could finish the sentence, SGT Copeland cut him off "Sorry chaplain, but that's a no go. I'm not crazy. Besides, once you go to CSC, the command is sure to find out. Then everyone thinks you're some type of crazy son of a bitch and life becomes hell. No thanks."

Danek was very familiar with this view of CSC, and although he knew it was largely unfounded, there was a kernel of truth in there as well. He had seen instances when a commander had reacted poorly to a soldier going to CSC. Even so, it was rare, and he very much wanted Copeland to at least be seen by a therapist for a brief evaluation.

The chaplain smiled " Yes, I've heard those rumors as well, Sergeant. But what I've seen, at least most of the time is that commanders are very supportive of soldiers getting the help they need. No different than going to a doc because your back is going out from too many road marches. Besides, the CSC has some very experienced therapists who could provide you with the sort of expert help you deserve. Moreover, it would be confidential."

Copeland was unmoved. "If I wanted a therapist I wouldn't be sitting here chaplain. And we both know that they don't keep things confidential the way you do. Thanks, but no thanks."

"That's fine. It's entirely your choice. In that case, let me tell you what we can do together to help you out," Danek replied. He then went on to explain some of the ways they could try and reduce the sergeant's anxiety. After reviewing these they agreed on a couple of things that Copeland could start to do right away.

Danek, however, was uneasy with the agreement. Although the sergeant was distressed by the unrelenting anxiety he was experiencing, *he had also become somewhat accustomed to living with his worries. At least most of the time. It wasn't clear whether his current discomfort would be sufficient to motivate him for the hard work of fighting his fears. He might simply decide that he could "tough it out" as he had been doing for much of his life.*

The best he could do, Danek concluded, was to continue to provide specific strategies that worked most of the time when soldiers gave it their best effort. Giving the sergeant an effective battle plan against anxiety, along with as much support as he could muster, would have to suffice. Ultimately, it would be up to the sergeant to put in the effort, and when dealing with anxiety it always took more effort than anyone realized at the beginning of treatment. He opened his calendar and made a note to drop by and see Copeland the next day.

ANXIETY: A BRIEF OVERVIEW

There are many types of anxiety disorders, including phobias, Obsessive Compulsive Disorder (OCD), panic attack disorder, post-traumatic stress disorder (PTSD), generalized anxiety disorder (GAD), etc. (National Institutes of Mental Health, 2017b).

Not surprisingly, at the heart of each of these disorders, is an individual's experience that his/her fears do not objectively match the threat they face. For example, an individual with a social phobia may be confronted with the need to give a presentation to a dozen co-workers. While many people may feel some discomfort as they worry about being well organized, clear, and making a good impression, the person with social phobia will respond with an experience of dread, heart palpitations, thoughts of being humiliated, and so on. In many cases, these fears will be so severe that the person simply refuses to give the presentation.

This excessive worry, usually accompanied by unrealistically negative thoughts and physiological symptoms (i.e. sweating, increased heart rate, tightening of muscles in neck and shoulders), is typical of anxiety disorders.

A discussion of every major anxiety disorder goes beyond the scope of this manual. Fortunately, for our purposes, there is little reason to conduct such an exhaustive review. By examining two of the more common anxiety disorders you will be able to develop the basic skills needed to respond to most forms of anxiety found in soldiers who seek your help.

There are two anxiety disorders we will look at in the following pages. These include Generalized Anxiety Disorder (GAD), and Post Traumatic Stress Disorder (PTSD).

GENERALIZED ANXIETY DISORDER (GAD)

Identifying And Responding To Generalized Anxiety Disorder

Generalized anxiety disorder (GAD) is seen in people who struggle with persistent, unrealistic, and excessive worries. The focus of these fears is most often about everyday events and situations that most others find to be of little concern (Bystritsky, Khalsa, Cameron, & Schiffman, 2013). The person with GAD, however, tend to expect the worst about the day to day challenges that may arise. As a result, these people experience an exaggerated and often intense sense of worry throughout their day. This occurs despite the lack of objective reasoning for the concern or at least none to warrant the intensity of their concern. The specific focus of their worries are varied and may include their health, family, job performance, evaluation by others, etc. There is no one specific concern, but rather a tendency to worry about any number of things. (When the worry is isolated to only oneor two issues, the disorder is likely to be diagnosed under a specific phobia, or if concentrated on social interactions it is likely to be diagnosed as social anxiety.)

GAD generally shows up in three ways:

- Thoughts centered on the expectation of negative consequences in one's life, often of a catastrophic nature
- The emotional experience of anxiety and occasionally dread
- Physical symptoms of stress that may include headaches, gastrointestinal distress, muscle tension, heart palpitations, etc.

It is not necessarily the case that the anxiety manifests itself in all three domains, but it will certainly be demonstrated in the affective and cognitive realms.

The person with GAD is generally perplexed by why he has these persistent concerns, and often (not always) recognizes that the fears are out of proportion to the reality of the situation he faces. Frequently one hears them say "I'm just a worrier", but this sort of self-reflective statement is more likely to be uttered by women than men, probably because men find it less acceptable to be worried. It is important to keep in mind that the person with GAD most often feels at a loss to how to stop worrying, and very frequently assumes it is something with which they must learn to live.

Approximately 3% of the adult population meets the criteria for GAD, with women being twice as likely to be affected as men (McLean, Asnaani, Litz, & Hoffman, 2011). Most often this form of anxiety emerges between childhood and middle age, and there is no clear precipitant that causes its onset. Although the cause is not clear, there is good evidence that several factors play a role – genetics, stressful life experiences, and family background (Bystritsky, Khalsa, Cameron, & Schiffman, 2013). Like most psychological disorders, GAD occurs across a spectrum ranging from mild to severe. At the mild end, one finds that people can function well, enjoy healthy relationships, and hold down jobs. At the more severe end of the spectrum, GAD can result in grossly diminished job performance, severely impaired relationships, and clinical depression.

As a reminder, when reviewing the symptoms for GAD listed below, please keep in mind that this is not an exhaustive accounting of the symptoms required to make a diagnosis. The list is provided simply to help you identify the general area of concern that deserves your attention.

The soldier who is struggling with a general anxiety disorder will present with at least three or more of the following, and at least some of these symptoms will have persisted for at least six months or more (American Psychiatric Association, 2020). If all of the symptoms have arisen only in the past six months, then the disorder is likely to be much more transient than GAD. This is a good prognostic indicator suggesting more robust functioning (as opposed to a chronic struggle with anxiety). Even so, how you would attempt to help the soldier is likely to be very similar even if the symptoms are of a shorter duration.

1. *Restlessness or feeling keyed up or on edge*
2. *Being easily fatigued*
3. *Difficulty concentrating or mind going blank*
4. *Irritability*
5. *Chronic tension*
6. *Sleep disturbance (difficulties falling asleep, staying asleep, or restless and unsatisfying sleep*

Course Of Generalized Anxiety Disorder

If left untreated the person with GAD is likely to continue to struggle with this disorder for years, and oftentimes for their entire life. Moreover, GAD typically first appears in young adulthood.[1]

---

1   Generalized Anxiety Disorder, Harvard Health Publications. June 2011.
    http://www.health.harvard.edu/newsletter_article/
    generalized-anxiety-disorder

When treated, however, the rate of success is very high (Bystritsky, et al, 2013). Both psychotherapy and medication have proven helpful in dealing with GAD. As is true with most disorders, the impact of these two approaches differs in certain important ways. Medication generally works much faster in reducing anxiety, and depending upon the specific medication used can show immediate effects.

Psychotherapy, however, results in an individual learning new coping skills and changing how they view themselves, others, and the situations that they fear. These new skills and perspectives result in the person having the ability to deal with anxiety over their lifetimes, generally without a reliance on medications. Improvements with psychotherapy generally take several weeks before an individual begins to see marked improvements. This assumes, of course, that the person is motivated to follow the therapist's recommendations.

With two effective but very different approaches to take in dealing with anxiety, the question arises as to which one should be utilized – medication or psychotherapy? The answer to this question depends upon the particulars that face the anxious person. For instance, if a soldier comes to you and is so anxious that he cannot perform his job then medication is preferable. If, however, the soldier is still performing well yet his anxiety is significantly impacting his mood and overall wellbeing then psychotherapy would be preferred. Of course, nothing prevents a treatment team from offering the soldier the chance to use both approaches at the same time. Indeed, it is not at all uncommon to treat anxiety with medication and psychotherapy (Bystritsky, et al, 2013), and once sufficient progress has been made in learning new coping skills the medication is tapered off.

Assessment of Generalized Anxiety Disorder

Assessing for anxiety should be straightforward. The first step is to remain aware of the general way in which the soldier presents himself while he is interacting with you. Is eye contact good? Are his movements fidgety and restless (such as frequently tapping fingers on the chair, shifting in his seat, rubbing his hands over his face/head, stuttering, etc.)? Is his train of thought clear or does it wander from one topic to another? Is his tone of voice normal or strained? All of these qualities easily observed and important to note.

As with every assessment, it is important to develop a rapport with the soldier. He has come to you with a goal in mind, and using the typical skills of a chaplain to explore that goal will go a long way toward putting him at ease. Only after having established an interest in helping the soldier with whatever goal he presented would you move on to make a pointed assessment of anxiety. An easy way to transition into these questions is, to begin with, a comment that goes something as follows:

> "I'm glad you came in to see me as it is clear that you have a lot to deal with right now. I know that many soldiers with these sorts of challenges can be affected in lots of ways so I want to ask you a little about that. For example, I'm wondering, given all of this stress, how has your sleep has been?"

When the soldier responds you can then delve further into his response. If he says, "My sleep is as good as ever," you would want to inquire further. "That's good. But tell me more about that... for example, how many hours of sleep do you usually get each night?" Even if he tells you 8 or 9 hours, you might follow up by asking how long it takes him to fall asleep. This normally is no more than 15 to 20 minutes (National Sleep Foundation, 2017). No matter what the response, it is advisable to ask for specifics regarding the quality of sleep, mid-sleep awakening, and whether the soldier requires any special means for falling asleep (e.g. does he consume alcohol to help himself fall asleep, take medications, etc.).

You would then proceed to ask about each of the six symptoms in a similar fashion. The more conversational the inquiry, the more likely you are to obtain helpful information. At the same time, do not hesitate to be direct. There is no point in pursuing the assessment if you do not obtain the information needed to clarify your understanding of the soldier's mental status. Although most chaplains will have no problem following up on each of the symptoms listed above, the following list of questions may be helpful.

Restlessness or feeling keyed up or on edge

- Do you often feel restless or tensed?
- How often does that happen?
- Is there a particular time of the day, or particular circumstances wherein you feel this way?

Being easily fatigued

1. What is your energy level now compared to what it was six months or a year ago?
2. Does this lack of energy seem to occur every day or just sometimes?
3. How often do you feel you lack the energy that you should have?
4. Does your lack of energy keep you from doing things that you would otherwise do?

Difficulty concentrating or mind going blank

- How often do you seem to have a problem concentrating, or getting easily distracted?
- Is this something that you've always had or is it something that you've especially noticed over the past six months or during the last year?

- Can you give me an example of when this happens?

Irritability

1. Everyone gets upset or irritated with others from time to time. Do you find yourself getting irritated with others from time to time? (The answer should be "yes" since this is the norm).
2. How often does this happen?
3. Has it happened more frequently over the past six months, or perhaps over the past year?
4. Does it seem to happen over things that you later, when thinking about it some, consider being small or unimportant matters? That is, things that did not warrant being that irritated about? Can you give me an example or two?

Chronic tension

- Everyone feels tense from time to time, but during certain stressful times in life, many of us will feel tense throughout much of the day. Rather like something is bothering us, something in the background of our day that weighs on us even when we are not thinking about it. Does this happen with you?
- Can you describe this tension for me, help me see it from your perspective?
- Do you feel this tension rarely or most days?

Sleep disturbance (difficulties falling asleep, staying asleep, or restless and unsatisfying sleep

- You've described some challenges that would upset most of us. Sometimes these sorts of stressors, quite naturally, make it more difficult to fall asleep – or, for that matter, more difficult to stay asleep. For some soldiers, I've known they simply say that they sleep throughout the night but do not sleep well. That is, they wake up still feeling tired and not very well rested. Do you have any of these sorts of problems with sleep?

- How much sleep do you get each night?
- How long have you been getting by on that many hours of sleep?
- How long does it usually take you to fall asleep?
- Do you wake up feeling well-rested?
- Is there anything you normally do to get to sleep at night? Any routines you have, anything you take to help you sleep, that sort of thing?

Key Symptom Checklist For Generalized Anxiety Disorder

Restlessness or feeling keyed up or on edge
Being easily fatigued
Difficulty concentrating or mind going blank
Irritability
Chronic tension
*Sleep disturbance (difficulties falling asleep, staying asleep, or restless and
    unsatisfying sleep*

Chaplain Interventions For Generalized Anxiety Disorder

There are some things the chaplain can do to help a soldier with GAD. It is important to keep in mind, however, that this form of anxiety can be very challenging to resolve since it is so unfocused. There are not simply one or two things that the soldier is worried about, but instead numerous events and potential situations that occupy the soldier's thoughts and create worry. What's more, many times the worry is so ill-formed that it cannot be traced to a set of events, but is simply a global sense of worry and concern. This creates a situation wherein there is no specific target at which to aim. If, for example, the soldier was anxious due to an upcoming promotions board it would be easy to focus on what makes that event unusually anxiety-provoking. You would then work with him to tease out unrealistic fears, speak of more realistic outcomes, and discuss healthy ways to respond to the stress. But when the fear is detached from a specific stressor, it becomes very difficult to trace the unrealistic fears and to provide more realistic perceptions. Even so, one is still able to teach effective coping skills, those means by which a soldier can lessen the distressing impact of anxiety (Bystritsky, et al, 2013). It is also helpful to assess the soldier to see in what ways if any, he is responding to his stress with maladaptive coping (i.e. alcohol, pornography, promiscuity, isolation, etc.).

There is much, as a chaplain, that you can do to help a soldier who has a generalized anxiety disorder. Although it would be perfectly reasonable to refer the soldier with this disorder to one's mental health colleagues, this will not always be possible. In these cases, the following interventions will often prove helpful.

1. **Psycho-education:** Whenever you have concluded that a soldier has a particular mental health disorder it is a good idea to discuss this with that individual. Describing what you believe to be the general problem facing the soldier often has the effect of providing some measure of relief, and at times an added sense of control. The problem begins to take a sharper focus in the soldier's mind, and in some fashion, it becomes more understandable. When telling a soldier that you believe he has an anxiety disorder it conveys the message that what he struggles with is not unheard of, but rather a familiar problem that many others have faced. Moreover, it is a problem that has been researched and for which there is a great deal of

help. Within this context, it is much easier to instill within the soldier a clear expectation that things can get better, and with this comes greater motivation on the soldier's part to do those things that you are about to suggest.

2. **Deconstruct Anxious Thought Processes:** Help the soldier begin to see that his worries are not due to events pressing in on him, but rather the majority of his worries are due to his unrealistically negative expectations about those things he faces in life. To be effective, this requires that you gently question the soldier about his worries, how often his fears have come true, and if he believes that the dire consequences he imagines for himself are similar to those that others in his situation would expect. The answer is usually "No." The main point is to get the soldier to see that the worries are not tightly aligned with reality. There is precious little chance that such a discussion will cause him to express, with sudden surprise, "Gosh, I never thought of that! Now I'm not worried." But this conversation acts as a starting point, a beachhead as it were, from which other discussions will take place. Moreover, if the worries are out of proportion to the reality he faces, then they are also much more easily managed. (Note that they are *managed* rather than eliminated. You are unlikely to eliminate these worries, but making them manageable is a great advance for any anxiety sufferer).

3. **Separate Worry From Safety:** Help the soldier to focus on the relationship between worry and safety – there is none. For many people who struggle with constant worry, it serves a protective function. When they dwell on that which they have concerns about, they often believe (albeit often unconsciously) that they are less likely to suffer the dreaded consequences that are the focus of their worry. Thus, chronic 'overthinking' about worries become a habit since they have spent a good deal of time practicing this approach to life, and more often

than not the consequences they feared never materialize. Over time a connection is built between worry and safety. The worry acts as a sentry, always on guard, protecting the individual from the things that they imagine to be a threat. It is often helpful to point out that these worries have only caused them pain. The anxious person will often respond that this may be true, but they do not know at this point how to stop worrying. That's fine, and no doubt largely true. This gives you the opportunity to let them know that you have some ways that they can begin to diminish both the frequency and intensity of their worries. This takes us to the next point.

4. **Relaxation Techniques:** Teaching the soldier to relax is crucial. Many relaxation exercises have been developed by psychologists over the years (Manzoni, Pagnini, Castelnuovo, Molinari, 2008). It is not possible to go over these in this brief manual, but the main ideas can be summarized nicely. A person who is plagued with chronic worry can be taught to relax by sitting comfortably and taking several deep breaths. You should have them inhale deeply as you count to three and then, without holding their breath (we are not trying to get them to hyperventilate, which would be counterproductive), have them exhale slowly as you count to three. Repeat four to five times. Have them think of a relaxing scene while they practice this deep breathing. A scene that they have personally experienced before is preferable, but if needed they can make up such a scene. To be clear, it is a relaxing scene, not a memory of a party, sky diving, or other 'fun' time. The focus is on relaxing. This may be a time when they were walking on the beach, or while camping and laying under the stars, or sitting at their kitchen table on a fall day with a hot cup of coffee and feeling at peace.

ARMY CHAPLAIN FIELD MANUAL

The idea is to pair the relaxation of deep breathing with the scene of relaxing. Then have the soldier practice this on his own: preferably two or more times a day for at least five minutes each practice. While they are practicing with you, however, have them complete the breathing and spend several minutes quietly visiting this mental image. They should imagine the sights, sounds, smells, and feel of all that the scene encompasses. For example, with the beach scene, it would include the sand and the ocean, the sound of waves and seagulls, the feel of the warm sun and the sand under their feet, and the smell of the salt air.

5. **Identify Triggers:** Have the soldier begin to keep a diary of his anxiety and those times when he became most anxious, and the people and situations associated with these times. After one or two weeks it is often very clear that certain situations and people are especially prone to trigger anxiety. This allows you to problem-solve with the soldier on how best to avoid or diminish the impact of these triggers.

6. **Lifestyle Check:** Lastly, review any lifestyle habits that may be exacerbating the anxiety. This may include an over-reliance on caffeine (i.e., coffee, energy drinks), tobacco use, poor sleep habits, poor eating, etc. (Velten, Lavallee, Scholten, Meyer, Zhang, Schneider, and Margraf, 2014). People are generally resistant to change lifestyle habits, but if you can get the soldier to 'experiment' by changing just one of these for one week it may provide sufficient relief to motivate him to continue and to consider changing other habits as well.

Summary of Chaplain Interventions for Generalized Anxiety Disorder

Psychoeducation
Providing a reality check about the soldier's fears

Disconnecting the habit of worrying from feeling safe (so the act of
worrying does not provide a security blanket)

Teach relaxation skills

Identify triggers of anxiety

Recommend changes in the soldier's lifestyle that increase will reduce
anxiety

POST-TRAUMATIC STRESS DISORDER (PTSD)

*T*he deployment had started with all the usual frustrations that Chaplain Murphy had come to expect from his previous jumps downrange. But despite these difficulties, morale within the unit remained high and the chaplain was pleased.

This was his fourth deployment in seven years. Most chaplains would have wanted a break, but not Murphy. He was nearing retirement and the opportunity to serve soldiers in a theater of war was quickly coming to an end. The thought pained him. With all of his children now grown and busy pursuing their own lives, and his wife having passed away ten years earlier, he did not feel the same constraints about deployment as did many of the younger chaplains. Indeed, he very much wished he could fit in another "trip to the sandbox" after this one was completed before the Army let him go.

That was not going to happen, however, and the realization brought a sinking feeling to his gut every time he thought about it. Murphy consoled himself by remembering that he was lucky to have gotten the current deployment with the 10th Mountain Division. To be slotted for the current mobilization had taken persistence, friends in the right places, and luck (or perhaps, he thought, divine intervention). He would make the most of this last adventure.

It was Tuesday evening when Chaplain Murphy hurriedly made his way into one of the DFACs at Bagram Air Base. It was a sprawling complex at the northeast corner of Afghanistan, located about 25 miles from the city of Bagram. The chaplain had a Bible study to lead in 45 minutes and very little time to grab some dinner.

The DFAC was an oasis of air-conditioned bliss. July had been a hot month with average temperatures hovering at 105 degrees. Although August was showing the typical cooling pattern, the chaplain was not impressed with a mere drop of two or three degrees. He had grown up in northern Michigan where "heat waves" of 85 degrees sent everyone scurrying to the lake.

Having quickly loaded his tray with some roast beef and potatoes, the chaplain hurried to find a place to sit. Spotting a group of familiar faces Murphy slid into the seat next to a young soldier named Johnson. He was 24 years old, formerly an infantryman who now worked in the TOC. SGT Johnson could be mistaken for a high school sophomore, and his baby-faced appearance had earned him the unfortunate nickname of "Gerber," a homage to the baby food brand.

Murphy enjoyed sharing meals with Johnson. He was good company. Most often when Murphy sat down at the chow hall with Johnson the Sergeant would greet him with a big smile, then look around the table at his fellow enlisted men with feigned disgust. A moment later, with a slow Southern drawl, he would loudly exclaim "Hey boys, it's time to clean it up. Chappy is here and he doesn't need to hear any of your low life trash talk."

But today, Johnson seemed preoccupied. As Murphy talked with the other soldiers he noticed that SGT Johnson's concentration was focused on a group of foreign nationals who were serving food and cleaning tables. When another group of soldiers bursts into loud laughter Johnson flinched, then quietly checked that the M4 he had placed on the floor next to his chair was still there. It was a momentary reaction from which he quickly recovered but Murphy noticed. There wasn't alot that escaped the old chaplain's attention.

Johnson looked over at the chaplain and shrugged self-consciously. "Just a little on edge today," he explained. Nodding, Murphy asked, "Had some tough missions lately? Heard they've been sending you outside the wire quite a bit."

Johnson gave a dismissive wave of his hand. "Not that tough, Padre. You know, just supporting a couple of bases. No combat missions..." Johnson's voice trailed off for a moment as he looked away. "Those missions are a thing of the past for me now. I'm good."

Murphy wasn't convinced but decided to lighten the conversation for a moment. "Looks like your Braves got lucky against the Pirates" Murphy teased.

"Oh Chappy, don't start with me. There's no way the game should have lasted that long. But the main thing is the best team walked away in triumph. You know what I mean? By the way, Chappy, what have the Tigers done lately?"

Murphy shook his head before answering. He was thinking the kid is really off his game asking me that question. Must not be following what's happening in the majors anymore.

"You mean when they crushed the Indians?"

Johnson momentarily looked surprised, then trying to recover replied, "That's it? A win against the Indians? Yeah, I knew they won that game, but hell, my grandma could beat the Indians." The chaplain laughed. Typical Johnson. And so it went, back and forth as they exchanged insults about their favorite teams, NASCAR drivers, fishing stories, and so forth. Throughout it all, however, Johnson kept scanning the DFAC, looking on edge, and paying special attention to the foreign nationals.

Johnson was one of those soldiers that stood out from the crowd. Murphy had known him since he transferred into the unit three months before deployment. Johnson had joined the Army upon graduating from high school and according to the commander had been an outstanding soldier. He was dependable, smart, easy-going, and could get others to do what needed to be done by example. But in a previous deployment, when on patrol, his squad sustained three KIA. One of these was his CHU mate. Johnson's reaction to those losses was typical: sadness, anger and a growing resolve to get the job done. By the end of that deployment, however, four more soldiers in his platoon had been severely injured. With each casualty Johnson began to show more and more stress.

During the last month of that deployment, Johnson had been wounded, and medevac'd to Landstuhl Germany. Although he eventually made a full recovery, putting the stress of that deployment behind him was much more difficult. Indeed, the command had offered him the chance to pass on the current mission, to stay in the rear and support the unit from their base back home. Johnson would have none of it, pled to be deployed, insisting he was "ready to roll."

Driven by a conviction that he owed it to his fallen comrades to get back into the fight, he became relentless. Against all odds his persistence paid off. The command eventually conceded. With an important limitation: he would deploy, but it would mean working in the TOC. Combat missions we're out of the question. The sergeant jumped at the chance.

Looking at Johnson now Murphy began to worry. This was not the easy-going young man he had first met back in Fort Drum. Yes, he was able to exchange social pleasantries and banter about baseball, sports, and what not. But in spite of that, Johnson was clearly on edge, and fervently trying to hide his anxiety.

Murphy had an idea. "I just thought of something. They opened a new coffee shop on base, one of those Green Bean joints. I've been meaning to check out their brew. Care to join me sometime?" Johnson chewed through a piece of bacon before answering. "Coffee? If you're paying it would be my privilege to accompany you on that outing chaplain."

At 1800 that same evening Chaplain Murphy knocked on CHU 68 in Section C of the base's Army quarters. Then he waited. After half a minute he knocked again and Johnson opened the door, squinting hard against the sun beating into his face. He looked as though he had just woken from a nap.

"Got time for some coffee, Sergeant" Murphy said brightly. "Remember this morning?"

"Oh, yeah, that's right. Um, you know, Chappy it's been a long day, been ripping and running at the TOC and thought I might catch some Z's right here in my personal Shangri-La."

Murphy was not to be dissuaded. "Come on Johnson, I would love the company and I promise not to preach... not much anyway." The sergeant looked a little sheepish as he replied "Is this an order?" Murphy smiled but remained silent.

After a long pause Johnson resigned himself to the situation. "Guess this is one of those "voluntold situations", so yeah, sure, I would love to grab a cup of coffee."

The Green Bean coffee shack was a five-minute walk from Johnson's CHU. Surprisingly, the place was nearly empty. They grabbed two cups of coffee and walked outside to sit under the camo netting. After some small talk about the unit, and the things Johnson most wanted to do when he returned stateside, Murphy asked the sergeant how he was doing with the deployment. "Seems like everyone in the unit is stressed, how are you holding up?" The sergeant smiled, then looked away. The chaplain persisted, and Johnson began to open up.

He described feeling constantly on edge, frequently "checking his six." Although the sergeant had struggled with hypervigilance for some time, it had lately gotten even worse. Johnson also spoke about nightmares wherein scenes of past combat engagements were replayed with vivid reality.

Murphy was puzzled. "Wonder what's different? What's changed?" "I know you were already tense, but now things are obviously a whole lot worse."

Johnson squinted and considered whether he should give an honest answer. "Well" he began, drawing a deep breath, "You heard about the IED up in Kandahar that killed five of our guys?" Murphy had heard. The men were part of 1st Battalion, 10th Mountain Division. They were patrolling

44

over the Montreal Bypass when their MRAP hit an IED. A big one. Powerful enough to blow off all the doors as well as the turret.

" *Yeah, I know about that... breaks my heart* " *the chaplain said soberly.*

"One of those guys was my buddy," Johnson continued. "We went through basic together. Would hang out you know, shoot pool, even got to know his family a little..." Johnson's eyes began to water. He stopped talking, coughed, then rubbed his eyes. "This damn sand gives me allergies."

Murphy felt confident that he now had the key to what was happening with Johnson. He had seen it before: a soldier with PTSD gets back in the fight, struggles a little but keeps it together. Then something goes sideways that pulls him back into the dark hole of PTSD. For Johnson, it was the death of his friend that pulled the trigger.

"Hey, let's finish this coffee over at the chapel. We can get away from this sand for a bit." The sergeant looked relieved and immediately agreed.

Once inside the chaplain's office Johnson spoke more freely about what he had been experiencing, admitting to feeling constantly on guard and in a state of high alert.

"It's sort of like I'm never able to get out of my patrol mindset. I'm on base but always keyed up, kinda like a firefight is about to break out. Just never know when. It's just a really weird time, Chappy," he confided. "I'm fine, don't get me wrong..." he trailed off before attempting to diffuse his discomfort with a joke. "Probably just knocking back too many Red Bulls."

Murphy laughed " Yeah, those things can string you up pretty tight, but I think it might be a little more than Red Bull that has you feeling this way."

"I know, but I would hate for it to go any further than you and me. They might send me home, and I'm not ready for that. I can still do my job. I can. I'm not just giving you a bunch of BS either."

"No, I don't think you're trying to fool me" Murphy chuckled. "Well, except when you go on about the Tigers. Listen, I know you're a squared away guy, but you're shouldering a lot of stress. Sometimes it helps to take a breather, like we did today, to sort things out. You might find

it helpful if we made it a habit, at least for a little while, to talk about this stuff once in a while. Deal?"

SGT Johnson hesitated for a moment, then asked "Is that another order?" Seeing the chaplain's surprise, he added "I'm joking with you sir. Sure thing, drop by my CHU anytime you like. We can talk. I don't know if it will help, but worth a try. Just promise me you won't keep bringing up that sorry excuse for a baseball team you keep going on about every time we have chow."

Identifying and Responding to Post Traumatic Stress Disorder

In 1980 the American Psychological Association recognized a special form of anxiety, one that was precipitated by a traumatic event, and resulted in an individual behaving and feeling as though that horrific event might reoccur at any moment (Friedman, 2016). Because of the clear link between trauma and the subsequent onset of severe anxiety (stress), the disorder was named Post Traumatic Stress Disorder (PTSD). Research has shown that PTSD occurs along a spectrum from mild to very severe, and can be brought about by a number of different events: sexual and physical abuse; natural disasters such as hurricanes, tornadoes and earthquakes; social conflicts including riots; domestic violence; and, perhaps most well-known of all, the brutality of combat.

It is important to note that not all people who are subjected to the same stressor will find it traumatic (National Institutes of Mental Health, 2017b). A group of 10 people could be riding in a van that crashes, resulting in significant injuries for each member. In all likelihood, some members would have some degree of PTSD as a result of the crash. They would find that certain sights, sounds, and/or smells associated with that van ride and a crash would trigger significant anxiety reactions. But another group of people involved in the same accident might show little, if any, long term reaction to the incident.

What this demonstrates is that one cannot assume toomuch when diagnosing PTSD. For some people, events that you or I might consider psychologically traumatizing seem to them to be only a challenging situation. Conversely, others may react with pitched anxiety to events that you or I would think to be mere hardships, but certainly nothing of a traumatizing nature.

Now, this is not to say that the concept of "traumatizing event" is infinitely malleable such that a soldier could mention that his mother once upon a time failed to butter his toast and he has forever since suffered as a consequence of the trauma of unbuttered toast. It does, however, show that "traumatizing event" is a concept heavily weighed down by the patient's subjective appraisal of the situation that is thought to be traumatizing.

This becomes even clearer with the following example: Imagine three soldiers in a field hospital that has come under attack. One of the soldiers has just finished surgery and has not awoken. He hears and sees nothing of the gunfire, mortars, screaming, etc. The second soldier, having come in earlier with a compound fracture of his tibia, has been given a powerful pain killer. Due to this medication, the soldier is euphoric, and although he sees and hears the attack and defense of the base he does not find it upsetting. Now there is a third soldier present who does not have the benefit of being comatose or having medication-induced euphoria. Instead, he simply came in to have a skin rash looked at, hoping for some sympathy and medication to provide relief. This soldier also sees and hears the attack, and recognizes the very real danger that the base will be overrun.

This example illustrates that the most important factor in the traumatizing impact of an event is how it is understood by the one who lived through it. Only the last soldier in the example above is likely to be at significant risk for experiencing PTSD because only he perceived the situation as a threat to his health/life. The takeaway is that it is not possible to diagnose PTSD unless the person has experienced an event or situation that he found extraordinarily threatening (American Psychiatric Association, 2020). Having established this as a starting point, we need to look at the other aspects of this disorder.

There are three primary symptoms of PTSD that may occur after experiencing trauma.

1. Re-experiencing the trauma
2. Avoidance
3. Hyperarousal

Let's briefly look at each of these in turn.

Re-experiencing the Trauma

This symptom is typically manifested in nightmares, intrusive frightening thoughts, and flashbacks (Bartoszek, Hannan, Kamm, Pamp, & Maieritsch, 2017). When considering whether nightmares are related to the trauma, one looks at whether the individual has a history of nightmares. If the soldier frequently had nightmares prior to the trauma, then the fact that he continues to have nightmares does not suggest a relation to PTSD. The exception to this is if the nightmares now focus on the traumatic event. On the other hand, if the soldier had been relatively free of nightmares before the traumatic event, then the fact that he is now experiencing them should make you wonder if this is related to PTSD. It is important to note that the content of these nightmares may not be clearly related to the stressful events the soldier has experienced. Of course, it is much clearer if they do correspond to the trauma, but the fact is that PTSD may express itself with generally increased fear, even in one's sleep, and this need not be related to the trauma.

Flashbacks are another form of re-experiencing the trauma. A flashback occurs when memories of the trauma return, generally unbidden, and take on an unusually vivid quality. At times these memories are so vivid that the soldier feels himself pulled back into the event as though reliving the situation once again. In its most extreme form, flashbacks will result in a soldier momentarily losing the sense of his current surroundings. When this appears the soldier may stare without focusing, fail to respond to what is said to him, and look frightened or expressionless. This is the most extreme form of flashbacks and is by no means typical of all individuals who are struggling with PTSD.

Frightening thoughts frequently intrude on the soldier with PTSD. These may directly relate to the traumatic event, but more frequently involve safety concerns more generally (Perusini, 2015). For example, one soldier who had acquired PTSD after being severely wounded in a firefight in Iraq returned to the theater two years later. Due to his injuries, he no longer went on patrols but instead had a job in the TOC. Nevertheless, he frequently became anxious when seeing local Iraqis working on base even though they invariably were accompanied by armed soldiers. He would discuss in detail the possible ways in which the Iraqis could overpower the soldiers and then go on a murderous rampage. At times the anxiety this gaverise to caused him to immediately come to Combat Stress Control for help in reducing his anxiety. These thoughts and fears had been absent in his prior tour, beginning only after he was injured in the firefight (the traumatizing event).

Avoidance

Avoidance here refers to attempts to avoid anything that would give rise to anxiety. Of course, most individuals prefer not to be anxious so it is not unusual for soldiers to avoid that which would bring about this experience. For the person with PTSD, however, this avoidance goes beyond what is typically found. Those things that remind them of the traumatic event may be assiduously avoided (Thompson & Waltz, 2009). If the soldier was hit by an IED while riding in an

MRAP, he may avoid those areas on base where there are MRAPs. If the soldier was involved in a mortar attack that destroys the DFAC in which he was having chow, he may begin to take his meals elsewhere and so forth. Additionally, they may experience "emotional numbing," wherein they feel very little at all.

Hyperarousal

When an individual has been traumatized it is not unusual for them to remain on "high alert." That is, they tend to consciously, or unconsciously, remain on guard against future threats to their safety (Institute of Medicine, 2014). This is frequently seen in soldiers who are easily startled, constantly on edge/tense, have difficulty sleeping, and experience angry outbursts with little provocation.

The course of Post-Traumatic Stress Disorder

The course of PTSD varies. For one to be diagnosed with PTSD, the symptoms we've reviewed must be present a month or more after the traumatic event. Moreover, the symptoms usually occur within three months after such an event, but there are times when the soldier will not begin to experience these difficulties until many months later (and there are some reports, although very rare, of soldiers first experiencing PTSD symptoms years after the event (Frueh, Grubaugh, Yeager, & Magruder, 2009). For those who do struggle with this disorder, the course of their symptoms may abate within six months or so, but for others, it can become a chronic condition. Those who are accurately diagnosed and receive appropriate care are much less likely to have this become an issue that plagues them over the long term.

On a final note, it is important to recognize that PTSD occurs over a spectrum from mild to severe (Iribarren, Prolo, Neagos, & Chiappelli, 2005). For some soldiers on the mild end of the spectrum, it will simply be a challenge with which they find ways to successfully deal as they move on with life. For others, at the end of the spectrum, it will become a debilitating condition that impacts the entire course of their life. Obviously, as with most mental disorders, those individuals who have many strengths (i.e., good social support, stable family life, good adaptive skills, higher IQ, etc.) generally do better than those who do not enjoy these strengths.

Assessment of Post-Traumatic Stress Disorder

The assessment of PTSD would appear to be straightforward, and yet for a number of reasons it can be rather challenging. For one, when it occurs on the mild side of the spectrum, the soldier may function fairly well, and the symptoms that one associates with the disorder may be largely masked by the soldier's ability to effectively cope.

Strong coping skills are to be valued, so when this is the case the prognosis is all the better. Nevertheless, it makes your task of discerning when PTSD is present all the more difficult. Another reason why PTSD may be hard to detect is that a soldier may have multiple mental health issues (Brady, Killeen, Brewerton, & Lucerini, 2002). That means, when such a soldier comes to speak with you there could be a confusing mix of symptom. For example, it may be that the soldier is depressed, but having seen several friends die as a result of an IED, he also has PTSD. The depression, which may have already existed, worsens. Symptoms of depression – poor sleep, ruminations about various hardships, being socially withdrawn, reluctance to socialize, and persistently negative expectations – cloud the diagnostic picture.

A confusing number of symptoms is common, not unusual. Even so, a working diagnosis can usually be made. There are three main features of PTSD (as discussed above) to be kept in mind: re-experiencing the trauma, avoidance of reminders of the trauma, and hyper-arousal. An acronym to help remember this trifecta of symptoms is RAH (i.e., re-experiencing, avoidance, and hyperarousal).

Key Symptom Checklist for Post-Traumatic Stress Disorder

Re-experiencing the trauma
Avoidance of any reminders of trauma-related experience
Hyperarousal (increased caution, hypervigilance, constant tension, irritability, mild paranoia)

Chaplain Interventions for Post-Traumatic Stress Disorder

The effective treatment of PTSD generally takes the form of having the soldier "re-experience" the traumatizing event (s) while at the same time remaining in a relaxed state. At first glance, this would appear to be counter-intuitive. One often hears people say that they think it best if the trauma can simply be forgotten. There surely is wisdom in this sentiment, but the problem for the person who suffers from PTSD is that they cannot forget the event. They often put great efforts into doing so but generally to no avail. Indeed, many PTSD sufferers will go to great lengths to forget and take destructive paths to find such relief. This occurs by self-medicating with excessive use of alcohol or the illicit use of prescription drugs; other times it takes the form of promiscuity and at other times extreme and frequent risk-taking (Leeies, Pagura, Sareen, & Bolton, 2010).

This is not to say that all who suffer from the effects of PTSD turn to these coping strategies, far from it, but many do. Most often these methods simply lead to greater troubles, and the person ends up more miserable than ever. What is needed is to have the soldier face the trauma with calm and confidence. To do this, he or she must not avoid remembering the traumatizing events but instead make a concerted effort in therapy to recall them in detail. The general name for these approaches is "exposure therapy" (Iribarren, et al, 2005).

The problem with PTSD is that it is very difficult to forget the trauma, and the mind's manner of dealing with those memories is to maintain the protective response of being on high alert for the danger to re-occur. How then does remembering the situation lead to a resolution? This is where the "state of relaxation" aspect of therapy comes into play. Because it is impossible to be both relaxed and on high alert (or anxious/guarded), one wants to have the PTSD sufferer first learn the skill of putting himself in a state of mental relaxation (Scotland-Coogan & Davis, 2016).

Once this is learned, and that state is achieved, the person begins to recount the trauma. As he speaks of these troubling events and remains relaxed, the old pairing of trauma memories and subsequent anxiety is slowly broken, and a new pairing is formed – relaxation in the face of these memories (Tuerk, Yoder, Grubaugh, Myric, Hamner, & Acierno, 2011).

You should expect that everything will not be smooth sailing as the therapy moves forward. At times the soldier's state of relaxation breaks, anxiety builds and it is necessary to momentarily stop the retelling of the trauma. Indeed, this sort of pattern is the norm. Nevertheless, by such fits and starts the story unfolds over time with greater detail, and less distress. Such therapies often proceed very slowly, for many months and sometimes up to a year. Despite the gradual nature of this treatment, it is without a doubt the approach for dealing with PTSD that is most strongly supported by research (Ogrodniczuk, Taylor, Thordarson, Maxfield, Fedoroff, & Lovell, 2003).

Unless a chaplain has extensive training in mental health it is not reasonable to expect him to engage a soldier in exposure therapy. Moreover, this form of therapy is certainly not appropriate for the field (Wangelin & Tuerk, 2014), although working with a soldier who is on base for an extended period would be fine.

So what can a chaplain do in this instance? Referral to Combat Stress Control is the first choice. At the CSC they will be able to determine if the PTSD is mild enough to be treated with anxiolytics (anti-anxiety drugs) which may allow him to continue in his present duties until returning to home where more intensive help would be available. Of course, they will also be able to decide whether the soldier should be taken from the field due to the impact of PTSD on his performance and judgment. Although most soldiers detest the idea of leaving the field under these conditions, in severe cases it is the best option both for the soldier and those that depend upon him to perform his duties with undivided attention. The impact of PTSD on a soldier's performance has nothing to do with his desire to fulfillhis duties, but operates independently of the soldier's will and is in no way a reflection of his character.

If the soldier refuses to seek help at CSC despite your best efforts to convince him (no doubt this discussion will include the impact on his career, which most often is negligible), then the chaplain has two courses of action. If you feel that the soldier is placing himself or others in dire jeopardy by continuing in his duties then calling his command is recommended. Many chaplains will see this as a betrayal of the soldier's trust. Inasmuch as it is not my intent to review the ethical contours of this predicament, I will simply point out that the issue of trust extends to those other soldiers that may be harmed or killed if the soldier with PTSD is allowed to function in some critical capacity in which he is no longer able to adequately fulfill his duties.

An example comes to mind of a young medic whose PTSD symptoms were so severe that during foot patrols in Iraq he would at times lapse into the belief that he was back in Afghanistan, surrounded by insurgents. Fortunately, he very clearly understood that despite his best efforts, he had become a liability for all those who counted upon him. In this instance, he found relief to be removed from the field, as he feared not only for himself but for the soldiers who lodged their trust in his ability to fully function in his capacity as a medic.

The last point to be made regarding what a chaplain can do in this regard is to offer support, provide guidance on how to avoid situations that trigger PTSD reactions, and teach common coping skills. An understanding chaplain can provide a great deal of relief to someone who feels very much alone and misunderstood due to the effects of PTSD.

Identifying the situations, sights, smells, interactions that cause a soldier to re-experience past trauma is also helpful. Knowing what triggers the reaction makes it easier to avoid those provocations.

Lastly, teaching the soldier how to relax when off duty will be of help as well. That might involve time alone, listening to music, exercising, getting extra sleep, reading, involvement in sports, etc.

If the soldier continues to refuse to contact CSC, and he is nearing the time when he will return home, be sure to encourage him to seek help once he arrives stateside. If he does not want to receive help from military resources there will be many private practitioners that can help. With a little effort, it is often possible to contact stateside resources before the soldier returns home, and in this way facilitate his transition into professional care. Military One Source (see "Resources" section) can be very helpful in this regard. So too can the chaplain's colleagues who are still stateside, and if the soldier is willing, his family can begin to arrange for professional care prior to his return.

Summary of Chaplain's Interventions for Post-Traumatic Stress Disorder

Referral to Combat Stress Control

Education about the military's policies regarding PTSD, the impact on career advancement, the support by others he is likely to find, etc.

Coordination with the soldier's command when the individual's safety, or that of others is jeopardized. Confidentiality is to be maintained, however, per Rule 503 of the Military Rules of Evidence. This requires the chaplain to obtain explicit permission for such coordination. The service member may also benefit by having you act as his or her advocate. Examples of such advocacy include having the soldier remain deployed but in a different capacity, or conversely to be sent stateside for treatment. Your effectiveness as an advocate will often be enhanced if you can consult with professionals within the Combat Stress Control.

Educate the soldier on the symptoms and course of PTSD Establish a point of contact with CONUS mental health professionals to assist soldiers upon his return.

DEPRESSION

*L*TC Bloom was an interesting soldier. He had grown up in a broken home where both parents were alcoholics and unemployed. Despite these hardships he was determined to make something of his life. While growing up, he often heard about his grandfather who had been a highly decorated Marine in World War II. Because his grandfather lived on the other side of the country they only met on a few occasions. Even so, the memories of these times together, and the stories his grandfather told of adventures in the Pacific, had carved a profound and indelible impression on his psyche.

Although Bloom was seldom seen in chapel services, and the likelihood that he would show up for a Bible study was less than that of a Green Beret taking up ballet, he had consistently been one of the most helpful officers in the unit.

Prior to joining the Army, the lieutenant colonel had been an enlisted in the Air Force working as a paralegal. When his AF contract was complete he made the unusual choice of joining the Army joking that he now "Wanted to know what it was like to live on the other side of the tracks." When asked, "Then why not the Marines?" He joked that he wanted to keep the family name untarnished within the Corp.

After transferring to the Army, Bloom went on to earn a bachelors degree in business management. Shortly thereafter he received his commission as an officer.

Even though he had not planned on making the Army a career, it turned out that he was doing so: with fifteen years of service to his credit it seemed foolish to get out. In fact, he often said that the Army was the one thing in life he could count on. It gave him structure, and a sense of purpose that he had never known before.

Unfortunately, his wife and children found military life more of a burden than a blessing. The frequent moves invariably caused a great deal of distress, and the fact that LTC Bloom insisted they live on base caused his family to resent what they saw as his lack of concern that they have something of a 'normal' life.

Over the years the stress continued to grow at home, and unconsciously LTC Bloom coped by throwing himself more and more into his work. The chasm that has been building between he and his family continued to widen.

The home front problems of LTC Bloom were vaguely familiar to Chaplain Gunderson: on a small base it was difficult to keep things secret for a very long time. It made matters worse as the LTC's wife had made her complaints known to many of her friends, who in turn talked to their husbands. With this "insider" information in mind, the chaplain had become concerned when he noticed Bloom's mood and behavior change over the past several months. The LTC was clearly going through a rough patch.he seldom laughed, no longer joined others for chow, constantly stayed late at the shop, and frequently appeared distracted and preoccupied.

The chaplain struggled with how to be of help. Gunderson cared deeply about the men he served, but he also had a natural sense of reserve. He was cautious about pushing himself into the lives of others unless explicitly invited.

Good fortune, however, intervened in the form of the Army Physical Fitness Test. Gunderson always made it a point on APFT mornings to arrive early so he had time to mingle with the soldiers in his unit. By the time he walked into the large cavernous hall, where the first part of the test would take place, several groups of soldiers were already huddled in clusters.

The jumbled noise of laugher mixed with dozens of conversations filled the air. "War stories" were being recounted about best – and worst – APFT efforts from the past. Most of these tales of former glory were punctuated with ear splitting profanity. More creative soldiers added graphically lurid details, undoubtedly intended for the amusement of the audience rather than historical accuracy. But even the most vulgar story was quickly sanitized the moment the chaplain joined the group.

Gunderson could not help but smile. It amused him how the men changed their habitual way of talking when he was nearby. Happily, he thought to himself, they continued to enjoy themselves even in the absence of the profanities. In fact, there was an almost festive atmosphere among the unit.

Yet, within this loud and cheerful crowd LTC Bloom sat off by himself. The chaplain decided that this was as a good an opportunity as he would ever have to check in on Bloom. He casually strode over to the LTC. Bloom looked up as the chaplain drew near and gave a tired smile. "Hey, Chaplain, how are things going in the soul saving business?"

Feigning hurt, Gunderson replied, "Not so good. Not good at all. Seems like there is one colonel in our unit that is afraid to step into chapel. Any ideas on how I might make some headway there?"

"Sure thing," Bloom said with a crooked smile. "Football and beer will get me through the door every time!" For the next few minutes they continued with light hearted banter. The conversation then turned to rumors of deployment, force reductions, and miscellaneous scuttlebutt.

Gunderson was about to suggest that they have lunch that afternoon when a large muscular staff sergeant boomed, "I need everybody to the line. NOW!" Push-ups were about to commence, and the time for talking had passed.

For the next hour and a half the APFT ground forward until the last soldier crossed the two-mile finish line. Gunderson had been in the final group of soldiers to run and was relieved to be done with the APFT for six more months. He was also surprised by his performance: 60 push-

ups, 70 sit ups, and the two-mile run in 19 minutes and 30 seconds. "Well, not great, but I passed" he thought to himself while re-lacing his running shoes.

Straightening back up, he spotted LTC Bloom who was standing with his hands on his knees trying to catch his breath. "What's up Colonel? Still trying to outrun those kids?" Bloom was well known for being more fit than most of the younger soldiers in the unit. It wasn't something he put too much stock in, but it did give him a little island of satisfaction. As long as he continued to score 300 on these fitness tests, he reasoned, the slow advance of 'Father Time' was nothing to worry about. This morning Bloom was looking forlorn.

"Not this time. Not even close. Guess my age is finally catching up with me." They began walking off the track, heading back to the gym where they would shower and get ready for the day. "Chaplain, I could have used a little prayer from you this morning. Seemed to have lost my mojo. I can't even catch a break at the APFT."

"Really, what do you mean?"

"Out of gas is what I mean. Seems like nothing is left in the tank. Two miles in eighteen minutes. Come on, I'm usually a sub-sixteen. But what should I expect..." Bloom drifted off. Then, without prompting he went on "I mean, these days I have a hard time even getting out of bed and dragging myself to work. Maybe I need to get some of that protein powder or whatever it is those kids are always gulping down."

"Hey, it's just an APFT score right? I mean you passed, so no big deal."

Bloom attempted a smile. "I guess. But it seems lately that if something can go wrong then I can be 100% certain it will. Today was supposed to be easy. I always smoke these things. Too easy as a matter of fact. Well, whatever... just one more thing on my growing list of screw ups. Can't wait to see what's going to happen with my OER this year. Probably get slaughtered."

Gunderson decided this was a good time to probe a little. "Sorry about the tough patch you're going through. I've noticed you've seemed sort of preoccupied lately. Like something is on your mind. From what you've been telling me, it sounds like you're getting pressed in on all sides."

Bloom raised an eyebrow. The chaplain quickly continued "Not that I've been intentionally watching you. I'm not a stalker!" he added for some levity. "But I think nearly anyone would notice that you've been distracted and have sort of isolated yourself. The engaged and happy guy I know has started to look pretty unhappy."

"Well Chaplain, those cheerful days of the past are not so easy to drum up anymore" Bloom responded. He then quickly added "But I'm happy enough, trust me. Really. Just tired."

When the chaplain remained quiet Bloom added a short explanation "Hey, have you ever had to deal with insomnia Chaplain? I mean for weeks at a time?"

"No. Not really," Gunderson answered honestly. "Maybe a few nights of staying awake thinking about problems in the church, something like that, but I wouldn't call it insomnia."

" You're lucky. It really messes with you." Bloom looked like he was about to speak again, then paused before striking a lighter tone. "Listen, I'm good to go. I've run into some tough weather so to speak. No big deal, you don't have to worry about me. I'm an old dog that's happy to just soldier on."

Gunderson thought about this for a moment. Bloom was not the sort of guy who wanted to talk about his personal problems, but clearly something was weighing on him.

"I'm not worried. Let's just say I would like to help, and from what you're saying it sounds like you could use a hand. Maybe we could grab lunch later today. Who knows, I might even be able to help you raise that disappointing APFT score by the next time we get tested."

Bloom smiled. "And you call yourself a chaplain! Kicking a guy when he's down. My run may have been in the tank, but I seem to recall crossing the finish line ahead of you."

ARMY CHAPLAIN FIELD MANUAL

Gunderson chuckled, "Hey, just think of me as the embodiment of tough love. Sounds like that's a 'yes' on lunch?"

Bloom rolled his eyes "Sure chaplain, lunch is good. If you can help me find a way to get some sleep I'll publicly announce that you are a miracle worker."

Gunderson considered this a victory. If the LTC would talk to him about his insomnia there was a good chance he would also open up about other things that were on his mind. Like the worries that were causing his insomnia.

"My modesty would prevent me from having you do that Colonel, but knowing you might someday hold me in such high esteem is touching. Not so touching as to let you beat me the next time we are on this track, but really, it tugs at my heart."

The LTC smirked good naturedly. " You know, maybe you really can help me with insomnia Chaplain, because clearly you're terrific at dreaming. And that's the only place you'll ever cross the two-mile mark ahead of me... in your dreams!"

Both men laughed and continued to walk back to the gym.
Chaplain Gunderson smiled to himself. He had never thought of the two-mile run as a mission field. From now on he would be sure to keep in mind that maybe, just maybe, a soldier will lower his guard after exhausting himself in a foot race.

Identifying and Responding to Depression

Depression is a term that most people are familiar with because it is frequently used to describe one's mood. You undoubtedly have often heard someone who is facing a challenging time in life say something to the effect of, "I guess right now I'm just feeling a little depressed about all of this." Or you may have heard others comment, "Oh, now that's really depressing." But what these comments point to are not the sort of depression we will be considering in this section of this book. What those statements (and similar statements) refer to are momentary periods of time when a person is rather sad, disappointed, or melancholy.

When a therapist refers to someone as depressed, however, they have something much more severe and much more specific in mind. Indeed, therapists try to be very specific regarding depression, and therefore divide this concept into various subtypes such as major depressive disorder, dysthymia, cyclothymia, etc. (Kessing, 2007).

You should also keep in mind that depressive symptoms may occur as featured in other disorders. For example, one may have a psychotic disorder with depressive features, an Adjustment Disorder (to be described later in this manual) with depressive features, and so forth (American Psychiatric Association, 2013). People who sufferfrom anxiety also often have depressive features due to the stress thatcomes with severe anxiety. In sum, depressive features are depressingly common in many disorders.

Although depression has many facets, most of these are easily identifiable – you will not have a difficult time identifying the depressed soldier if he is willing to be candid in answering your questions.

Not surprisingly, the main features of depression begins with a depressed mood. In addition those who have severe depression typically experience "anhedonia," which is a fancy way of saying that there is a lack of interest in events/people/hobbies that had in the past been enjoyed by the soldier. Related to this symptom is another, a tendency to become more socially withdrawn. Not surprisingly, such individuals often have difficulty in concentrating, sometimes to the extent that their job performance is compromised. A lack of self-esteem frequently is seen in those who are depressed, and this is most often thought to be a result of all the other symptoms that haunt the depressed individual.

There is another class of symptoms that need to be looked at, and these are called *vegetative* (related to functions essential for life). The list is rather short and includes a lack of energy being common among those suffering from a severe depression. This will most often be seen in general fatigue. Changes in appetite are common (both increased appetite as well as a lack of appetite... it varies from individual to individual). These changes are generally accompanied by changes in weight. Disturbed sleep is frequently seen and may appear as insomnia, restless sleep, or a need for longer periods of sleep. A diminished sex drive is also common.

Course of Depression

Depression is one of the most prevalent mental disorders found among adults with a twelve-month incidence of approximately 6% of the population struggling with depressive symptoms.[2] Women are more likely to be depressed (8%) than men (5%).[3]

According to a review of the research by Gadermann, Engel, et. Al., (2014), 13% of service members with a history of deployment meet the criteria for Major Depressive Disorder. This is nearly identical to the number of service members who experience a Major Depression while in a deployment (12%).[4]

Many of those who are depressed also suffer from anxiety (approximately two thirds). Moreover, soldiers who have a history of childhood trauma are much more likely to become depressed and anxious as adults.

When depression arises in conjunction with an anxiety disorder, it is likely to last longer than if it were the sole mental health issue.[5]

Although the course of depression is quite variable, research suggests that 70% of depressed adults recover within a year of the

---

2   https://www.adaa.org/about-adaa/press-room/facts-statistics).
3   http://www.nimh.nih.gov/health/statistics/prevalence/major-depression-among-adults.shtml
4   https://www.ncbi.nlm.nih.gov/pmc/articles/PMC4100466/
5   http://www.ncbi.nlm.nih.gov/pubmed/21294994

onset of symptoms.[6] Of those who are still depressed at the end of the first year, many (approximately 12%) will remain depressed up to five years later. Early intervention is crucial, although it should also be stressed that it is never too late to make significant changes that result in the resolution of depression.

Depression may develop gradually, or rather quickly. At times it can be traced to specific events in an individual's life such as the loss of a loved one, or a series of significant misfortunes (e.g., divorce followed by the loss of a job followed by a major move that puts trusted family and friends on the other side of the world). Conversely, it may develop gradually with no specific event being easily identifiable, but instead there is a steady decline in the individual's mood and reduction in healthy ways of thinking and behaving which in turn accelerates the depressive decline.

Assessment of Depression

Clinical depression goes beyond simply being gloomy, but rather to be significantly depressed nearly every day for several weeks or more. Individuals experiencing a severe depression will often say that they feel empty, hopeless, that the world has no color, etc. The most straightforward way to assess for depression is to speak in a straightforward manner with the soldier about the various symptoms listed above. Such an interview strategy would involve simply asking the soldier to describe his mood, and then follow up as to how long he had felt that way and how frequently he feels that way.

Each of the other symptom clusters mentioned earlier are similarly addressed in a straightforward, albeit conversational manner. At times it may take some probing to be sure you are getting a clear picture, but in general the process should not be difficult. When you

---

6   file:///C:/Users/Peter/Downloads/CH69_1009-1016%20(1).pdf

have completed that process, you should have a good idea of whether the soldier you are working with is depressed.

In addition to a depressed mood, there is often a lack of interest in those things that used to interest them – family, jobs, hobbies, sports, etc. This is called anhedonia and it is easily assessed by asking what the soldier does for fun, or what activities he is involved in that interests him and bring him pleasure. If he responds that very few, or no activities are of interest, then you should ask if there was a time when that was different. In this way you are comparing the soldier's current status to what he normally experiences, and to determine if this is a change from his baseline. If so, a diagnosis of depression is more likely.

A lack of energy is frequently seen in such instances, and a change of appetite is not uncommon (look for weight loss and weight gain). Sleep is frequently disturbed, and this can manifest itself in having problems falling asleep, staying asleep, or being sleepy much of the time.

Feelings of worthlessness and diminished self-esteem are also very common in part because when one is depressed it becomes more difficult to perform well on a day-to-day basis. It is easy to see that in light of the impact, chronically low energy and disturbed sleep have unhealthy effects on performance. Indeed, a lack of focus/ concentration is yet another symptom of depression, and related to these same challenges. The last symptom to be mentioned is that depressed individuals are often socially withdrawn. Moreover, this lack of social interaction has a tendency to exacerbate the depressive symptoms (Cacioppo, Hughes, Waite, Hawkley, & Thisted, 2006), making it a critical area to examine.

Just like many other psychological disorders, depression can take many forms, and this can make it difficult to accurately diagnose at times. By keeping the central features of depression in mind, however, the task is greatly simplified and making an accurate diagnosis becomes much easier.

Key Symptoms Checklist for Depression

Depressed mood
Anhedonia (lack of interest in events/people/hobbies)
Lack of energy
Changes in appetite
Low self-esteem
Disturbed sleep
Diminished focus/concentration
Social withdrawal

Chaplain Interventions for Depression

When working with depressed soldiers there is so much that a chaplain can do to be of help. Indeed, there are so many ways to effectively help the depressed individual, but we will only be able to review some of those that are most easily applicable, and effective.

1. Empathic Understanding

One of the first steps is to make a determination as to what has precipitated the depression. This is important for several reasons. The first of which is that a soldier will be more motivated to receive the help that's being offered to him if he believes the chaplain understands him. There is a body of research in psychology showing that patients who feel understood, and clearly cared about, are much more likely to make therapy gains than those that feel otherwise (Ardito & Rabellino, 2011; Cronin, Brand & Mattanah, 2014). Working with chaplains is no different.

Another reason for determining the source of the depression is that you may be able to help the soldier develop a solution to the problem that has given rise to his distress. Clearly, there are many situations that arise where a solution is not possible: the source of distress will remain. Even so, knowing what this is, how it came about, and how the soldier has responded so far (both adaptively and less adaptively) is important in order to understand the context of the soldier's depression.

2. Challenging Distortions

If the source of the depression is something that that cannot be changed, such as a divorce, separation from family during deployment, a lost opportunity, etc., then you will want to find out how the soldier thinks about this event. For many who suffer with depression, such events are thought of in very unrealistic terms (Beck & Gellatly, 2016). A divorce, for example, is not simply thought of as a huge loss, and the painful end of what was once felt to be a life affirming relationship. The extremely depressed soldier is likely to also feel extreme self-condemnation, and view the future as hopeless. The divorce might be viewed, for instance, as a reflection of the soldier's lack of worth, or that happiness will now forever be out of reach. It is these extreme thoughts that the chaplain must be aware of, and to which he must eventually respond. It is important, however, to start by patiently hearing the soldier out. You want to be able to view the world from his perspective. Only then can you effectively begin to gently question whether his catastrophic conclusions are realistic.

Your goal is not to talk the soldier out of his strongly held perceptions. Instead, you want to engage him in examining whether these perceptions are realistic (Morrison, 2009). This takes time, patience and persistence.

Once a soldier begins to admit that his thoughts are not realistic, and recognizes that they are overly catastrophic, you'll want to have him begin to push back against them on his own. It won't do to only have these thoughts challenged during those times when you meet together. The most effective approach requires that he also does this whenever these ideas arise during the week (which they surely will). The more one takes the initiative and actively attempts to refute this sort of thinking, the better the outcome will be (Keithly, Samples, & Strupp,1980).

3. Scheduling Positive Activities

From what was discussed previously about the symptoms of depression you will recall that depressed individuals often fail to stay involved in activities that had been of interest in the past. A very powerful means for helping soldiers begin to feel better is to have them resume activities that they enjoyed in the past (National Institute of Mental Health, 2016). Some soldiers will object, saying that these activities no longer interest them, so there is no point in pursuing such activities. Simply explain that although you realize this is true, it is also true that if they force themselves to do the activities it is very likely that before long they will once again derive pleasure from being so engaged. If the soldier tells you that this does not "fix" the problem that has triggered the depression, you only need to reply while stating the fact that you are not attempting to fix the problem, but you are only trying to help the soldier become less depressed. You may also wish to add that when the soldier's depression lessens,he will be all that much more capable of fixing the problem without anyone's help.

4. Increasing Social Activity

Most people enjoy being around others. Although the amount of social interaction that each of us finds optimal varies considerably, a lack of meaningful interaction is destructive to mental health. That is why the depressed person's withdrawal from social contact contributes so much to a downward spiral of greater depression, then greater isolation, leading to worsening depression (National Institute of Mental Health, 2016). (It should be noted as well, that when depressed individuals persistently act in a depressed manner, others slowly shift from being consoling to avoiding the individual, thereby increasing the social isolation).

Most people who are severely depressed will tell you that they simply do not wish to be around others. Sometimes they will say that they do not have the right energy to engage with others, or perhaps that they feel they would simply dampen the spirits of those that they were with. These objections need to be swept aside: not because they are without merit, but because the depressed individual can overcome these obstacles. Despite a lack of energy the soldier can make himself join some buddies for a meal, or play a game of cards. And despite the pervasive sense of depression that same soldier can behave in a happier manner rather than show his depression and subsequently 'dampen the spirits' of those around him.

You may be thinking that pretending not to be depressed is counterintuitive, and that one would want a soldier to be honest about his feelings. This is true to a point. You want him to be honest with you because that is the only way you will be able to help him. But with others, even with his closest friends, he needs to behave for the most part in a way that is far happier than he feels. If he does not, then what he fears will certainly come true as others will feel dispirited in his presence, and will ultimately avoid him. Moreover, by acting happy he is very likely that before too long he will begin to feel happier (Fredrickson, 2001).

5. Good Health Habits

Although this is an important part of good mental health generally, and overcoming depression more specifically, most of what needs to be said is derived from common sense, even if it is supported by research. What you as a chaplain want to look out for is that the soldier is getting plenty of sleep on a regular basis; that he is eating well (Forsyth, Deane, & Williams, 2015); avoiding a reliance on caffeine, energy drinks, tobacco, alcohol, etc.). In this regard it is best not to make the abstinence from tobacco or caffeine a divisive point of contention. You will do well to advise, and simply to inform of the adverse effects of consuming excessive quantities of these items. Keep in mind that you cannot debate someone out of a reliance on these habits. With regard to sleep, the same approach is recommended. However, most soldiers will not have a heartfelt attraction to getting too little sleep. Consequently, you have more latitude in pressing your point in this realm of functioning. It may help to point out that sufficient sleep will allow the depressed soldier to better recuperate and thereby allow him to access all those abilities that have helped him to deal with stressful situations in the past. Too little sleep will sap his energies, act as a depressant, and fog their judgement. Whenthis happens, depressed soldiers are likely to turn to nicotine and caffeine to prop up their deficient abilities, which ultimately leads to a greater reliance on these same sources. Ultimately, no one with depression will be able to consume enough nicotine or caffeine just to make up or what their lack of sleep, and depression is robbing them of, and they will be all the worse for their efforts. Even so, habits are extremely hard to break. If the soldier is not responsive, it would be ill-advised to consistently press on this matter to the point that it becomes a source of conflict. In this regard, keep your role as that of an impartial advisor rather than a determined advocate of abstinence.

6. Positive Psychology

From the field of "positive psychology," many powerful, yet simple interventions have been examined, and these has been shown by research to be effective in lifting the moods of individuals (Bolier, Haverman & Westerhof, 2013). Positive psychology is that branch of the behavioral sciences that focuses upon the sorts of attitudes, habits, lifestyles, and thoughts that cause people to be happier and more resilient. Over the past decade, a wealth of research has found many ways in which people can achieve a happier life - even people who are deeply depressed (National Institute of Mental Health, 2016).

Below I have listed three recommendations that are often very helpful in this regard. Of course the chaplain must proceed with vigilance to the soldier's reaction when suggesting these tasks.

Someone who comes to you with severe depression and is right away told that they should start to focus on what they have to be grateful for is very likely to feel that the chaplain has not really understood how much pain they are in. They may see you as simply minimizing their difficulties and telling them "Don't look so glum, look at all you have to be grateful about." Consequently, it is best to use these interventions *after* you've firmly established that you recognize the importance of the stressors, frustrations and doubts he has described. Then point out that there are some tried and true means for helping him not to focus so intently on these concerns, and that by changing this focus his mood will greatly improve.

Encourage Gratitude

Over the past years, there has been an accumulated rich and fascinating body of research showing that people who practice intentionally being grateful are much happier than those who do not (Sansone & Sansone, 2010). With this in mind, it is recommended that you suggest to soldiers suffering from depression that they keep a "gratitude journal." This requires very little. Basically, each morning the soldier is asked to write down two or three things for which he is grateful. Examples include good health, has plenty to eat, he is employed, has a family that loves him, is in good health, has opportunities for the future, friends, the deployment is coming to an end, he is engaged in important work, his commander is supportive, etc. Ideally, the items added to the list each day will be new, but if some repetition occurs, this is fine. The main point is that the soldier should be adding some new items to the list each day, even if other items are repeated. Upon going to bed, the soldier should review this list carefully as it grows into more and more things for which he has to be grateful for.

Helping Others

In addition to the research evidence regarding gratitude, there is a corresponding body of research supporting the proposition that reaching out to help others lifts depressive moods, and even combats anxiety to a degree (Jenkinson, et al, 2013). This is not surprising inasmuch as the act of helping other people draws an individual's attention to the fact that others have challenges that are great, or greater, than his own. Moreover, by helping these individuals the soldier naturally shifts his focus from his own problems to the problems of others. If you have this option available, it is certainly worth trying. Examples include assisting friends, providing guidance for those who may be stateside, and helping in chapel services. The exact list will vary depending upon the soldier and the specifics of the situation.

Prayer & Worship

There is a substantial body of research showing that people who have an active faith life enjoy a much more robust sense of wellbeing, improved friendships, and good mental health (Verghese, 2008). As a chaplain, this is something that you are in an ideal position to encourage. Praying with soldiers is a terrific start. Providing them with a few meaningful ways in which they can incorporate their faith into their daily routine will be very helpful. This may involve brief times of personal prayer, other times of corporate prayer/worship, identifying a few scripture passages that are meaningful to the soldier, attendance at Bible study groups, etc. It is important to take a measured approach in this regard. Some soldiers will already have a robust faith life and your task will be to simply affirm and encourage what has already been built. Others will have little experience in pursuing a life of faith, and your approach should proceed in a way that is mindful of this fact. Whatever the soldier's current state of faith is, encouraging its development can be an important means for bringing relief from depression as he comes to realize that the one who made the universe is vitally and personally interested in his welfare.

Summary of Chaplain Interventions for Depression

Extend Empathic Understanding.
Constructively Challenge Distortions.
Schedule Positive Activities.
Increase Social Activity.
Promote Good Health Habits.
Encourage: Gratitude.
           Helping Others.
           Prayer & Worship.

THOUGHT DISORDERS

*C*haplain Harris had seen SGT Smith attending chapel for several weeks now. He was tough to miss: singing loudly, off key, hands frequently raised far overhead with his eyes closed. Clearly a parishioner that enjoyed the service. What's more he always made a point of coming to see the chaplain after the service ended to let him know how much he had gotten from the message. A chaplain could not help but like the man. It was after SGT Smith had been attending for two months that he asked if he could be part of the worship band. Given that in this deployment (the chaplain's third) very few soldiers had stepped forward to participate in this way, it seemed like a good idea to see if he had any musical chops.

The standard Chaplain Harris had set for being part of the worship team was fairly modest. In fact, he would accept anyone that did not cause his small congregation to run for the doors. Maybe Smith could meet that standard he reasoned. The sergeant began to talk about the band he belonged to prior to joining the service. Nothing special, just a four-man group with a drummer, a keyboard, and two guitarists. He had been the lead guitarist. Not good thought the chaplain. Given how very far off key he sang, it seemed a little unlikely that his band had been a huge success. "Maybe that's what led him to leave the band and join the Army" Harris mused to himself.

"Let me play something for you," Smith piped up with enthusiasm.

"Sure, why not," the chaplain responded, pointing him to the band's instruments that were set up on the chapel stage. The sergeant picked up *an electric guitar, turned on the amplifier, and checked the guitar's tuning. After a minute, he slowly started to strum a James Taylor melody. "Passable" Harris thought. "He won't make a living from music, but he won't scare anyone away either."*

A couple minutes passed while Smith worked his way through Fire and Rain. Just as Harris was about to stop him Smith paused, a conspiratorial smile spreading across his face. A moment later he exploded into a remarkable rendition of Aerosmith's 'Dream On'. His fingers flew along the fretboard while his body rocked back and forth.

"That's fine!" The chaplain shouted over the music. Smith was oblivious. Eyes closed, body convulsing in near epileptic rhythms he carried on, lost in the music. "I said that's fine, you can stop!" The chaplain shouted more loudly, but Smith simply continued to play. Moving up to the stage, Harris calmly turned off the amplifier. To his great relief the sergeant stopped playing a moment later, slowly coming out of his music induced seizures.

"Sorry about that... I kind of get lost in the music," Smith said sheepishly.

"No worries SGT Smith. I think we can use a guy like you. Next Sunday I want you to talk to SGT Kleen who is the head of our worship team. He'll figure out how best to use your talents. You're really very good. I'm looking forward to having you join us."

And so he did every Sunday for the next several months of the deployment. Always on time, always agreeable to doing what SGT Kleen asked of him. Moreover, his skills with a guitar came to be appreciated by many of the soldiers who attended Sunday chapel.

After a time, Smith grew more comfortable talking with others, and he began to attend the Bible study that was held each Tuesday evening. It was after one of these Bible studies that he approached the chaplain and asked whether he thought it likely that the devil could take on different forms and make himself visible to people.

"I suppose. What do you have in mind?" Harris responded cautiously. The chaplain had so many conversations about the devil with parishioners

over the years that he now instinctively responded with some hesitation. Most of these discussions involved portrayals of Satan as having horns, a spiked tail, and holding a pitch fork. He cringed at the idea. Although he felt very certain that Satan was a genuine entity, he found that such conversations required a good deal of effort to help the parishioner develop a more mature understanding of evil. Right now he didn't feel up to the task.

Smith took a step closer and leaned in. Speaking with an intensity the chaplain had not seen before, he confided in having been haunted by dreams of menacing individuals lurking around his CHU. When pressed to give more details, it became clear that these so-called dreams occurred even when the sergeant was wide awake.

Harris was concerned. "Sergeant, I know you talked about these being dreams, but the way you describe these things sounds as though you were, at least some of the time, wide awake."

Smith took a deep breath and nervously rubbed his chin. "That's what I've been thinking too. But that would be crazy, right? I mean, they almost always happen at night, when I'm alone in my CHU. So I figured they must be dreams."

"Sure, that makes sense but the question is: Were you asleep? You're the only one that knows that for certain."

The sergeant looked even more uncomfortable, "As best I can tell I was awake. But how can someone see these things if they are awake. That's what I'm worried about. If I was wide awake then maybe this is the devil showing himself to me."

Harris's sense of worry was deepening by the moment. Although he had a meeting scheduled to meet with a young captain who was interested in being baptized, it would have to wait.

"Tell you what, Sergeant, let's go to my office for a minute and we can hash some of this out. I don't want you leaving here today without us understanding this a bit more, and figuring out how to turn things around and get the upper hand on what is bothering you."

The sergeant's eyes grew wide. "So you're thinking Satan may be coming for me after all? Damn! That's what's been worrying me Chaplain. It's got me twisted up and tense all the time like at any moment he is going to grab me. But I won't go down without a fight. This last time he showed up I already had my M14 locked and loaded."

"Woah. Hold on a second. I didn't say that.   Listen, I know this is scary, it would be for anyone, but I think we can figure something out that will be a lot more helpful than your M14," Harris reassured him.

"You mean an exorcism!" The sergeant excitedly exclaimed.

"I'm sure that won't be necessary. Let's take this one step at a time. The first thing to do is take some time, right now, to figure things out and get a clearer picture of what is happening with you. Then we can move forward. Find a solution. Something that works better than your M14 or an exorcism."

Smith agreed to move their meeting to the chaplain's office, and as he sat down in a chair across from Harris' desk he let out an audible sigh of relief. "Feels safe in here Chaplain. Like nothing can get to me in here."

"That's right, Sergeant. It's safe in here, and a good place to tell me everything you can about what you've been seeing. Not just in your CHU but anywhere else as well. For that matter, anything you may have seen or heard, that seems out of the ordinary. That could include things you experienced even before you joined the Army. I've got time, so fill me in and we'll figure out what to do."

After an hour of talking, Harris learned that the images SGT Smith experienced in his CHU were just a sampling of the strange experiences that were occurring throughout his day. Hearing people call his name when he was alone, feeling someone push him as he walked by himself to the gym,and being rousted out of bed in the middle of the night only to find his CHU mates fast asleep.

These sorts of experiences had been going on for a little more than a year, but had become more frequent since being deployed. Due to his fear of being thought crazy, the sergeant had kept all of this to himself. He was not taking medication, and he assured the chaplain that he was not "tripping on drugs."

With that information Chaplain Harris felt he knew enough to formulate a plan. "You're not crazy, although some of the things you've been experiencing must make you feel that way. I'm not certain what is causing all of this to happen, but from what you've told me I really don't think it is the devil that is showing up in your CHU, or calling your name, or behind any of those other things that have troubled you."

"What are you saying Chaplain?" Smith responded defensively. "You don't believe in the devil? Because I can tell you for certain…"

Harris interrupted him. "No. I believe in the devil. Absolutely. I just don't think he is showing up in your CHU. We can talk about why I think that, but the more important thing right now is to help you get rid of these terrifying images that keep popping up. Don't you agree?"

The sergeant nervously shifted his gaze around the small office before fixating on one of the sandbagged filled windows. He was having a hard time keeping eye contact and appeared to be drifting off into his own world.

"Smith, listen to me. I know you want my help, so I'm asking that as your chaplain, you trust me. I have some friends over at Combat Stress Control that we can talk to and get their help in figuring this out. They are good soldiers and they aren't going to judge you. Just help. That's it. They are just there to help. We could walk over now. I'll give them a call, let them know we are on our way, and by chow time this evening we may have a handle on this thing. What do you say?"

Smith's reaction was a surprise. "I'll go. Once. Just this one time. But you've got to go there with me. Those demons won't try anything with you nearby. But, uh, yeah, just one time to see the head shrinkers."

As they left the chapel and moved toward the clinic, Chaplain Harris could see that Smith had started to relax. They fell into a comfortable silence. Harris began to breathe a little easier. The sergeant's disclosures of psychotic thoughts had rattled him. He wasn't sure what he would have done had his idea of going to CSC been rejected. "Something to think about when the dust settles" he figured, and made a mental footnote to follow up. But for the moment, just getting Smith to the clinic was enough. He would put this outcome in the 'win column' of his deployment.

79

Identifying and Responding to Thought Disorders

Because the incidence of thought disorders in the general population is so small – approximately 1% (National Institute of Mental Health, 2017a) – and within our armed forces are smaller, yet at less than 1% (Cowan, Weber, Fisher, Bedno, & Niebuhr, 2011), this section will be relatively brief. The most common thought disorder is schizophrenia, and this can be divided further into several further subtypes (American Psychiatric Association, 2013). There are, for instance, those who have paranoid schizophrenia (where the predominant feature includes delusions and hallucinations of a persecutory nature). Others suffer with catatonic schizophrenia wherein the person's movements are drastically reduced, sometimes to the point of near motionless. Conversely, they may engage in seemingly purposeless movements. Then, there is the disorganized subtype wherein the person has significant difficulties organizing their thoughts to the point that simple activities of daily living are a struggle (e.g., getting dressed, feeding themselves, etc.). Effect in such individuals is often inappropriate to the situation, and their speech nonsensical. Still, other subtypes exist as well. With each subtype one must realize that a medical condition could be giving rise to the symptoms, therefore making consultation with a physician is very essential.

Schizophrenia is chronic and lifelong (National Institute of Mental Health, 2017a). The exception to this rule includes those whose symptoms have been brought on by medication, sleep deprivation, etc. These individuals, however, should not be diagnosed with schizophrenia inasmuch as there is a clearly identifiable external cause of their symptoms. Once the cause is removed (i.e., they stop taking the medication, are no longer sleep deprived, etc.), their psychotic symptoms abate.

Schizophrenia is one of the psychiatric disorders that has a clear genetic link (Owen, O'Donovan, & Craddock, 2005). If a parent is schizophrenic, their offspring have a 10% chance of also developing schizophrenia; if an identical twin is schizophrenic, there is a 40% chance that the other twin will develop this disorder (Gejman, Sanders, & Duan, 2010). The good news in these findings is that there is also a very large environmental component, and consequently genetics are not the absolute determiner of whether one develops the disease.

Course of Thought Disorders
(With a Focus on Schizophrenia)

As noted above, schizophrenia is rare, occurring in approximately 1% of the population (National Institute of Mental Health, 2017a). Although it sometimes begins as early as childhood, more typically the first signs are seen in late adolescence and early adulthood. From the onset, the majority of people who are afflicted show signs of the disorder sometime between the ages of 16 and 30 years of age; it is rare for someone to develop this disorder after the age of 45 years (Rajji, Ismail, & Mulsant, 2009).

Schizophrenia occurs along a spectrum from severe to relatively mild, the latter being when symptoms are manageable through medication and behavioral interventions, and the individual is able to live independently (Harvey & Bellack, 2009). For some individuals, symptoms remain fairly constant throughout their lives with little change in severity. For others, there is a gradual worsening until a steady state is reached some years later. Yet, others find out that symptoms fluctuate, sometimes severe, at other times mild depending upon the stressors they encounter and how closely they adhere to a proper medication regime.

Assessment of Thought Disorders
(With a Focus on Schizophrenia)

Symptoms of this disorder can be conceptualized along three dimensions: positive symptoms, negative symptoms and cognitive symptoms. Positive symptoms are those that are generally not seen in healthy people and include hallucinations, disorganized thinking where logic is grossly impaired, agitated body movements and delusions. Negative symptoms are those wherein certain qualities are missing. This includes 'flat affect' (and extreme absence of emotion), the relative lack of speech, having little pleasure in life's daily activities, and so forth. These symptoms may be mistaken for depression, and consequently one always looks to see if other symptoms (such as hallucinations) are also present.

The cognitive symptoms are often subtle, and these too can be mistaken for simple deficits in one's abilities, or the sign of another disorder. These include difficulty in focusing and deficits in being able to make decisions and understand simple information.

When considering whether a soldier may be schizophrenic, one must weigh the evidence that the symptoms are instead the result of drug abuse. Making assessment more difficult is the fact that those who are schizophrenic are much more likely to abuse drugs and alcohol (National Institute of Mental Health, 2017a). Although drug/alcohol abuse does not appear to cause schizophrenia, many who have this disorder tend to turn to these substances to "self-medicate."

A thorough history of the soldier's use of medications and recreational drugs is important in this regard, but complicated by the hesitancy of soldiers to admit to something that is not only frowned upon by society, but might result in a court martial. If you have any hope of finding the truth about the soldier's drug use, the establishment of a trusting relationship and clearly articulated limits of confidentiality are essential. As noted before, a medical evaluation is crucial.

There is a common misconception that people with schizophrenia are prone to violence. The fact is that this is rather rare. They do, however, commit suicide much more frequently than the general population who have a of suicide attempt rate of 0.6% (Center for Disease Control, 2015), compared with 5% for those with schizophrenia (Hor & Taylor, 2010). If you suspect that the soldier with whom you are working is at risk of committing suicide, be certain to perform a thorough assessment (see Suicide section later in this manual).

Key Symptom Checklist for Schizophrenia

Hallucinations (may involve any of the senses: visual, auditory, tactile, olfactory)

Delusions (beliefs, usually of a personal nature that have no basis in fact)

Odd behaviors (unpredictable agitation, bizarre posture)

Grossly disorganized thinking (often expressed through extreme difficulty completing tasks, including self-care).

Minimal speech or incoherent speech.

Chaplain Interventions for Thought Disorders (With a Focus on Schizophrenia)

As mentioned earlier, the key to effectively intervening with schizophrenic soldiers is medication management. This means that your primary objective must be to secure the soldier's motivation to consult with a psychiatrist who can do a thorough psychiatric evaluation, and initiate a medication regime to control and reduce symptoms. Some schizophrenic individuals are relieved to learn that their symptoms are not unique and that medications can help them find relief. Others, particularly those with paranoid features, will be exceedingly distrustful of consulting with a physician.

As it is often the case, the trust that the soldier puts in the chaplain makes all the difference in giving them the confidence to take the necessary steps to obtain more help. Keep in mind that the Combat Stress Control team is available for consultation in these instances, and you need not to identify the soldier in order to obtain such consultation. A good working relationship with CSC should be a priority for every chaplain inasmuch as these situations will arise on more than one occasion when you are in the field.

Although medication is the lynchpin of effective intervention with a schizophrenic soldier, other intervention will be employed as adjunctive services (Guo et al., 2010). One of the most important aspects in this regard is to enlist the soldier's help in managing his own symptoms.

When providing the soldier with psycho-education, it is helpful to frame the description of schizophrenia in a way that encourages self-observation and symptoms management (Patel, Cherian, Gohil, & Atkinson, 2014). Telling a soldier that schizophrenia is similar to other chronic illnesses helps to establish this mind set. Just as the person with diabetes must be aware of the foods that trigger certain reactions, and learn to respond accordingly, so also the individual with schizophrenia must learn what triggers his hallucinations, delusions, and any other symptoms (Patel et al., 2014). This may be family tensions, chronic lack of sleep, prolonged social isolation, etc. What's more, he needs to become aware of when his symptoms are first beginning to re-appear or become more pronounced. By having this awareness, the individual is able to work better with others to keep these symptoms to a minimum.

If the soldier has been self-medicating his symptoms through drug/alcohol abuse, this must also be addressed. Again, a referral to CSC will result in the proper referral to a rehabilitation program designed to remediate his dependency on recreational drugs and alcohol.

Cognitive behavioral therapy may also prove useful (Morrison, 2009). In this form of therapy, the soldier will be taught how best to question the veracity of their hallucinations and delusions when these symptoms are still mild (presumably after the initiation of medication). They can also learn how best 'not to listen' to voices in their head. CBT can be a powerful adjunctive means for giving the soldier the tools to maintain contact with reality.

Family education about schizophrenia is an essential component of effective treatment (McFarlane, Dixon, Lukens, & Lucksted, 2003). Clearly, this is difficult in the field if not normally impossible. But it is very likely that you will have the ability to communicate with the soldier's family through email, or by phone on one or two occasions. Even in these brief contacts, much can be done to help families begin to recognize what the soldier faces, and the support he will need. In these opportunities of contact with the family, a great focus needs to be put on encouraging them to seek out continued psychiatric help once he returns home.

One of the most critical things you can do is to provide a sense of hope (Barut, Dietrich, Zanoni, & Ridgner, 2016), both to the solider and their family, making it very clear that even though schizophrenia is a serious and lifelong disorder, there is every hope that he can have a rich and rewarding life if the intervention program described above is followed.

Summary of Chaplain Interventions for Thought Disorders (With a Focus on Schizophrenia)

Psychiatric referral.
Psycho-education & self-management of symptoms.
Drug/alcohol referral as needed.
Cognitive Behavior Therapy referral.
Family support.

ADJUSTMENT DISORDER

*C*OL *Simmons had stopped by the chaplain's office earlier in the day to talk about a young officer with whom he had become concerned, LT Joanna Blain. The lieutenant had joined the unit about a year ago. Although she had been an exemplary soldier, "a real pistol" according to the commander, her performance of late had been troubling. "Seems like she's phoning it in Chaplain. Not what I expect, and certainly not what the unit needs from her."*

At first Simmons had not been overly concerned. But as her performance continued to languish, he became uneasy. His impatience grew. She was new to the Army, fresh out of college ROTC. The colonel wondered if he would have to chalk her up as a "failure to adapt to military life." It happened sometimes. On the other hand, he reasoned, she may simply lack the skills needed to succeed at her position. That, however, seemed unlikely given her stellar academic performance and earlier success when first attached to the unit.

Whatever the cause might be Blain needed to quickly turn herself around. If improvement didn't happen soon, her military career would be shortlived. The LT had already received two counseling statements, and during the last one she came very close to admitting that she was not up to the task.

With this in mind COL Simmons decided to approach Chaplain Smith. "I've seen her in chapel from time to time," COL Simmons noted. "Any chance you've come to know her? Has she spoken to you about any problems she might be having? Because if something is going on with her she needs to find a solution, fast. We need someone in that position who can do the job. I'm hoping she can turn things around. But it better be quick. Otherwise she'll be relieved and reassigned."

The commander was an understanding man, but he was also a bottom line kind of soldier who was committed to mission first.

"Sure, I'm very familiar with LT Blain. She attends chapel and occasionally comes to Bible study. But as you know colonel, even if she had confided some problems to me I wouldn't be able to say anything about that to anyone else."

The colonel grimaced. "I know that, Chappy. I'm just wanting to know if you can run a little interference. She needs to get her head in the game sooner rather than later. I've cut her some slack, maybe even more than I should have, but I'm not her mother. Blain's got to start performing, or I'll get someone who can."

"Fair enough. I'll speak with her and see what I can do," the chaplain replied. Simmons paused for a moment looking as though he might want to say something more, then quickly turned and walked out of the office.

Chaplain Smith had grown accustomed to how the colonel ended conversations. Although he had a good heart, his social skills were that of a rhinoceros. Small talk in particular made him feel as though he were probing his way through a mine field. When he had said all that needed to be said the conversation simply came to a screeching halt.

Smith sighed and sat down behind his desk. He was surprised to learn that LT Blain was struggling. In all his interactions with her she had come across as smart and capable, having good insight and a dry sense of humor. She didn't talk about herself much, so the chaplain couldn't really say he knew her well. But from what little he had gleaned he thought her to be a high-speed soldier.

The following Wednesday night, LT Blain made one of her periodic appearances at Bible study. The conversation with the commander was still fresh in the chaplain's mind, and he paid close attention to the lieutenant. She seemed the same as every other time he saw her: quiet, attentive, reflective. Eventually, the study concluded and soldiers began to trail out of the chapel. "LT Blain, are you rushing off somewhere, or do you have a minute?" Smith asked.

"Actually chaplain I was heading back to the shop…" she let silence fill in the rest of her sentence. Smith smiled, remaining quiet and feigning ignorance as to the meaning of her response.

"But sure, yeah, I can stay for a few minutes longer."

"Great. There was something I wanted to run by you. Let's go to my office and we can sit down for a few minutes." He saw Blain's puzzled expression, but inasmuch as there were still some soldiers left in the chapel he did not want to explain the reason for his request. They entered the office, adjacent to the chapel, and sat down. Using as much tact as he could muster, Chaplain Smith related the recent conversation he had with the commander, leaving out the comments regarding how close Blain was to being relieved of her duties.

"So having heard what the commander said, I wanted to talk with you for a few minutes to see if there is something I can do to help. It just strikes me that the description the commander gave of your performance isn't consistent with the person I've gotten to know."

Looking much like a teen who had been confronted about a speeding ticket, LT Blain replied "Thanks, Chaplain. I appreciate your concern but I don't think there is anything anyone can do to help. I've just got to get more focused. I'll get it straightened out."

Without having directly told Smith to mind his own business, LT Blain had nonetheless clearly conveyed that she did not want any help. On the other hand, she hadn't made any moves to get up and leave. Perhaps, the chaplain concluded, the door for a conversation was still open. "Sure, I understand, and I don't want to intrude where I'm not wanted, but if I can help I would love to do so."

"Again, I appreciate your offer, but I can take care of this myself. I get it, I really do. The colonel has been very clear with me about how I've screwed up. And now he's even spoken with you about it, so I get it, things have to change and that's what I'm working on. Like I said, I'm headed back to the shop right now… gotta catch up on everything."

Well that's pretty clear, Smith thought to himself. "Bugger off" *was the message.*

But Smith wasn't convinced that the young soldier really did "get it" as she had said. "LT Blain, there is one more thing I should mention. Something of which you may not be aware. The commander also told me that things have gotten to the tipping point. He's talking about relieving you of your duties if things don't turn around soon. That's one reason I'm talking to you – I would hate to see that happen."

The change in LT Blain was immediate. She stiffened at the news, then slumped back into her chair. "I knew it had gotten bad. The counseling statements drilled that home, but I guess I was kidding myself that it had not gotten to this point. Relieve me of my duties! Wow. That just sucks.... Oh, uh, sorry sir."

"If you don't mind my saying so," *Chaplain Smith broke in,* "I think it's time to face this realistically. Whatever is getting in the way of your success needs to be resolved quickly. Let me help. I've seen too many soldiers go it alone when they didn't need to. That way of handling these things usually doesn't turn out very well."

After a moment of reflection, LT Blain said, "I really doubt that anyone can help with this, but sure...Let me tell you what's going on, and if you can figure out a solution then you really will be a miracle worker." *With that she began to tell her story.*

Her fiancé, Christopher, had abruptly ended their relationship four months ago. With the certitude of a surgeon's knife he had amputated and tossed aside her long cherished dreams of building a future together.

She did not understand how that could happen. They had been high school sweethearts, went on to attend the same college, and shared the goal of entering the military upon graduation. Getting married sometime along the way was a given.

During his senior year of college, however, Christopher's interest in the military began to wane. He had secured an internship at a private firm and was doing well. The lifestyle of the corporate world appealed to him more than he had imagined. The idea that he might someday be able to secure a job that provided money, travel, and influence was surprisingly attractive.

It wasn't long before Christopher decided to change his career plans. The military was out. He wanted to be in the world of big business. What's more, he wanted Joanna to be in that same world. After all, he reasoned, if she continued with her military plans it would add a great deal of stress to both of them when they did marry. How would he be able to establish himself as a leader in any company if had to pack up and move every few years?

Joanna, however, was resolute in her desire to have a military career. But neither would she give up on the idea that she and Christopher could both pursue their professional passions and remain together.

Exactly how this could be worked out neither of them knew. But there had to be a way.

Shortly after graduating from college Joanna entered the Army and Christopher began working at the same company in which he had interned. They lived a couple hours away from one another - close enough to spend most weekends together.

For the first-year things went well. Life seemed full of promise. Both of them were happy with their relationship, and excited about the future.

Six weeks before Christmas Joanna got news that her unit was to be deployed to Iraq. She dreaded telling Christopher, knowing that he would both miss her and worry about her safety. His reaction, however, was nothing close to what she expected.

"Wow. I guess I knew that would happen sooner or later, but the timing really sucks" he responded. "You see, I was offered a promotion. It's a big deal. Almost no one gets promoted this fast. If I keep this up I'll be in middle management in no time."

He went on to exclaim that he couldn't see himself waiting around "pretending to be a priest" while she was deployed. "I'm young and moving *up. I want you to be there with me. But if your Army career is more important to you than our relationship, maybe this whole thing isn't going to work out after all? Maybe it's time we faced up to reality."*

She patiently explained what he already knew… that a deployment was not a choice. "I'm an Army officer. I've made a commitment. If they tell me they need me to deploy then I deploy. That's the deal. You know that… but it doesn't mean we can't find a way to make this work. Lots of people make it work and so can we."

Joanna went even further and assured him that after she completed her initial service obligation she would transition to civilian life. If he would just be patient everything would work out.

He looked at her without emotion and explained, somewhat sternly now, that waiting for her was not an option. "You will have at least one more change of duty assignment. What am I supposed to do with that? Follow you? I'm sorry, but that's not happening. We've had a good run. Let's just leave it at that and wish each other well."

His mind was made up, his decision set: they would go their own ways.

"So that was the end of what I thought was a fairy tale romance" LT Blain concluded. "Instead of riding off hand in hand into the sunset I ended up single, and wondering where I went wrong."

She seemed remarkably calm given the circumstances. Chaplain Smith commented on her composure. "I'm done with crying" she responded. "Over the past couple months I've vacillated between feeling angry and apathetic. But the crying is over."

"How is your appetite and sleep?" The chaplain asked, thinking that she may be depressed.

"Not great, but not bad. I get my six to seven hours each night. Appetite? I don't get hungry very often but I'm smart enough to know I have to eat. The only thing different is feeling like I'm some middle-aged lady going through menopause. One hour I'm feeling down, and then the next hour I'm furious at my fiancé-- I mean, my ex-fiancé."

"Sort of messes with my concentration. Sudden onset of squirrel brain every once in a while" she ended with a sigh. "Guess I just need to push it aside and drive on. That's the Army way, right?"

Chaplain Smith smiled. "Drive on" was something he heard frequently, and it brought back memories of his youth when he was an infantryman. Someone falling out on a ruck march? "Drive on soldier!" Injured on a mission? "Drive on!" He could still hear the shouts of his NCOs as though it were yesterday.

He loved the idea of persevering no matter the challenges, but he also realized that some soldiers used the motto as a way to avoid dealing with life's big problems. " Yes. Drive on is right. But I wonder if you can push forward with your job duties while also giving yourself a little time to recover from this disappointment. I'm concerned that simply pushing yourself forward in the way you've been doing isn't working out too well. Maybe it's time to try a different approach. If you like, we could talk about ways you can find some relief, start to make sense of all this and begin to feel better about getting your life back on track."

Blain shrugged her shoulders. Smith decided to elaborate. "Let me put it this way: When you think back on all of this a year from now, you will want to say to yourself that you went through a very dark period in life and came out the other side stronger than before...with your Army career still intact. Are you willing to give it a try?"

LT Blain, looking skeptical, replied "Well... OK, let me hear what you have in mind. If it makes sense, then sure, why not give it a shot? It's got to be better than getting more counseling statements."

Chaplain Smith was happy. It was a first step. That night, before LT Blain headed back to her shop, they began the work of helping her heal from the heartbreak she had described, and rebuild both her life and career.

Identifying and Responding to Adjustment Disorder

Adjustment Disorder is given to individuals whose response to stressful life events are so severe as to be out of proportion to what is expected. What sort of life events might these be? The list is nearly endless, but some examples will give you a good idea: divorce, the illness of a loved one, moving to a different city, natural disaster (such as experiencing a tornado, flash flood, etc.), bankruptcy, incarceration, the death of a loved one, failing in a job or at school, and the list goes on. Of course each of these events is likely to produce stress in anyone, but for the person who is diagnosed with an adjustment disorder, the reaction is much more severe. How severe? Enoughthat the person's ability to effectively cope with what are called the 'activities of daily living' (ADL) are significantly impaired (American Psychiatric Association, 2013). These individuals are not simply stressed, but stressed beyond their ability to effectively cope.

Course of Adjustment Disorder

Research shows that people struggling with adjustment disorders normally return to their baseline functioning within six months from the time the initial stressor took place (Carta, Balestrieri, Murru, & Hardoy, 2009). It is important to note that the onset of symptoms must occur within three months from the time that the stressor first occurred. Because such stressors do not always have a definitive start, but instead may gradually develop (e.g., a deteriorating relationship with a spouse), this criteria can be difficult to accurately assess. This is not of paramount importance. What is more important is the fact thatthe stress the person is experiencing can be linked to some event(s), and that within a fairly short time their painful symptoms began to develop (American Psychiatric Association, 2013).

This particular diagnosis has not received much research attention, but it appears that many, perhaps most individuals with this diagnosis will eventually return to their previous state of functioning (Carta et al., 2009). This, of course, is good news. But it should not be inferred that attempts to effectively intervene are not important – reducing the amount of time a person is struggling to adapt can have a profound impact on his ability to limit the damage done by his being overwhelmed during this time. The loss of employment, friendships, and confidence to weather further stress all increase as long as the symptoms persist. In the case of military personnel, there is the very real risk that as long as the symptoms persist the individual will compromise his safety, or that of others, by his diminished capacity to carry out his job. Moreover, the progression from distress to suicidal ideation has been found to be faster for those suffering with an adjustment disorder than it is in other disorders such as major depression.

Assessment of Adjustment Disorder

Chaplains will frequently be faced with individuals presenting with these symptoms in light of the often unpredictable, frequently changing, and demanding circumstances under which a soldier operates. It is a good idea to become familiar with this diagnosis, and how best to make an assessment. Begin by taking note of new stressors that have developed in the soldier's life, or common stressors that have dramatically increased during the past few months. Deployment would be at the top of this list, and deployment during a time of family stress should cause you to take particular note.

Once this criterion is established you will want to see if it is in some way related to other symptoms mentioned above. In other words, if the soldier appears depressed, anxious, agitated, angry and so forth, were these mental states apparent prior to the stressor? If so, were they mild, or were they nearly as pronounced as they are during your assessment? If they have appeared since the stressor, or have significantly increased, then it is very likely that the soldier has an adjustment disorder. Keep in mind, however, if the soldier meets the criteria for another diagnosis such as major depression, or PTSD, and these symptoms are seen in that diagnosis, then adjustment disorder does not necessarily apply.

Why not? Because the other disorder is considered to better explain the symptoms. If this does not seem as clear cut as you would like, then consider yourself part of a large crowd – such is the state of diagnosing mental disorders.

The specific symptoms that fall under this diagnosis are varied. They include a depressed mood, anxiety, a sense of hopelessness, social withdrawal, somatic complaints (e.g., stomach pains, headaches, twitching, etc.), impulsivity, and agitation (American Psychiatric Association, 2013). Again, bear in mind that soldiers may present with any or all of these symptoms and still not be diagnosed as having an adjustment disorder. It is only when these symptoms are linked with a recent stressor and significantly impair the soldier's ability to carry out activities of daily living that this diagnosis is given.

Key Symptom Checklist for Adjustment Disorder

Symptoms that impair activities of daily living.
Onset occurs within three months of a stressor.
Symptoms are more severe than would be expected.
No other mental health disorder (i.e., major depression, PTSD, etc.) is present.

Chaplain Interventions for Adjustment Disorder

When faced with a soldier who is struggling with an adjustment disorder, you will often find out that certain maladaptive thoughts and behaviors have taken root that tend to keep the stress in place. For example, the soldier may have become more isolative due to his lack of interest in pursuing those social activities that in the past gavehim pleasure. The fellow who had enjoyed a game of cards with his buddies, or would go to the chow hall with friends, is no longer doing these things. The soldier may also have begun to focus so much on the source of his distress that he no longer pays adequate attention tothe good things that still remain in his life. It is easy for someone who struggles with an adjustment disorder to believe that this current state of affairs will last forever, rather than see it as a temporary challenge that must be worked through.

Consequently, you will want to examine how the soldier is responding to the stress, even beyond the assessment that determines if he meets the criteria for this diagnosis. This sort of examination will be critical in informing your decisions about how best to be of help. Each individual reacts differently to stress, and this is no different in those with an adjustment disorder. You will want to focus your attention on two main areas of functioning:

- How the soldier thinks about the stress and its implications.
- How he behaves in response to the stress.

Most individuals with adjustment disorder will unintentionally exaggerate the implications that the stressful event holds. For example, if he has been divorced while deployed, he may conclude that his life is over, and that no real happiness can be found in the future. In turn, he may have turned away from friends, or become overly dependent upon them and thereby driven some people away. He may also have become dependent on nicotine, energy drinks, or simply have spent all of his time working rather than taking enough time to relax.

These responses can be addressed by you – first by tactfully exploring these reactions so as to get as much information as possible, then by gently challenging his unrealistic conclusions. For the soldier in the example above, one would be cognizant of the very real pain and loss that accompany a divorce. This would be expressed to the soldier, but having done so you would want to better understand what he means by 'his life is over.'

Whatever his reply, you can be assured that the statement is an unhealthy exaggeration that can be tactfully challenged. Does this mean he can never find another woman whom he will love? The response is likely to be "Not someone like my wife." Although this may be true, it certainly does not mean he will not be able to find someone different, someone whom he loves just as much and returns this love with equal measure, and someone with whom he can share his life with.

Of course it is important, as always, to challenge these distortions in a way that does not minimize the soldier's real suffering. That will simply increase the chances that he fails to seek you out again. But do not make the mistake of failing to challenge the distortion either, as that too will eventually lead the soldier to conclude that you are rather a nice officer with whom to chat, but of no real use beyond that role. By combining affirmation/understanding of the soldier's very real stress and pain with a gentle-yet-pointed challenging of his assumptions regarding its impact on his life, you will reap the best of both worlds.

If you find that the soldier has stopped doing those things that gave him pleasure and a sense of belonging or purpose in the past, encourage him to resume those activities. It is often best to start with just one or two of the activities that have been dropped, and then add others in time. Many soldiers will let you know that they do not wish to resume those activities, and that they no longer receive pleasure from those pursuits. Do not be dissuaded. Simply explain that you do not expect him to immediately enjoy these things, but that by engaging in them gradually he will very shortly begin to find pleasure in them once again. Mental states do not trump behavior. On the contrary, as a general maxim, one's behavior trumps one's mental state. If you can get a soldier to behave socially, for example, it will not be long before the soldier feels much more sociable.

The effectiveness of medication is debated in regards to adjustment disorders. Some would argue it is of little use, others would point out that many medications can take weeks to see a significant impact, and then many more weeks to later taper off the medication. It is highly recommended that you seriously consider a referral to a psychiatrist if depression or anxiety are well pronounced.

Although medications will not 'cure' the soldier's concerns, they can be a tremendous help in allowing him to tap into those skills and personal strengths that have helped him in the past. Both depression and anxiety can block soldiers from accessing these attributes, so medication should be a consideration when either of these affective states are pronounced.

Summary of Chaplain Interventions for Adjustment Disorder

Identify the stressor that precipitated the adjustment disorder, and any factors that are perpetuating the distress (especially look for unrealistic conclusions about the future, or about the soldier's self-worth: also look for the subsequent development of poor sleeping habits, overreliance on caffeine/nicotine, etc.)

In a supportive manner, confront the primary cognitive distortions associated with the stressful event and its aftermath.

Help keep the soldier involved in activities that provide constructive social interaction, and still other activities that provide a sense of enjoyment and are meaningful.

Consider referral for psychiatric consult if depression or anxiety are severe, or the disorder prevents the soldier from performing his duties as needed.

As always, remain aware of suicide potential and perform appropriate assessment.

SECTION III

Less Common But Important Mental Health Concerns

INTRODUCTION

We have been looking at those disorders that you, as a chaplain, are most likely to see while working with military personnel. There are, however, a number of other concerns that will present themselves to you in the course of your work, and it is to these that we turn next.

My goal in the follow section is to help you gain a working familiarity with each of the topics listed below. Acquiring this knowledge will allow you to confidently and effectively respond when a soldier comes to you struggling with one of these issues. The topics that we will cover in this section include:

- Suicide Assessment
- Panic Attack Disorder
- Personality Disorders
- Response to Sexual Assault
- Drug and Alcohol Abuse
- Traumatic Brain Injury (TBI)
- When to Make a Mental Health Referral

SUICIDE ASSESSMENT
AND PREVENTION

*S*ergeant Provo worked in supply. He was a single father in the Army Reserves on his first deployment. When he initially joined the Army Provo dreamt of being an infantryman. Bad luck and an open contract, however, led to a very different MOS: Supply Sergeant. SGT Provo never fully adapted to this misfortune.

Upon first learning of his MOS he thought there had been a mistake. After being reassured that it was not an error, he became angry. He experienced it as a personal affront. Belittled. It never occurred to him that signing an open contract was a bad idea. That it left him vulnerable to be assigned to some MOS that he found demeaning. He had been naïve and simply assumed that nearly every soldier becomes an 11 Bravo.

His disappointment eventually grew into chronic bitterness. A permanent scowl creased his otherwise rotund face. He was fond of saying "The Army runs on supply lines. It's their life blood. I'm supply, and I make the Army run. Now f... off so I can keep the Army running."

Some soldiers concluded that his gruff demeanor was due to being a single father who had to leave his only child in order to go on this, his first deployment with the Army Reserves. Others simply thought him a naturally unpleasant person whose son was no doubt happy to have him away from home. Either way, the sergeant was reassuringly consistent in his demeanor day after day. Whenever someone from the unit needed something from supply Provo responded as though it was a painful intrusion on his personal time and resources.

Need additional cold weather gear? Might want to think about buying your own – or suck it up and embrace the cold weather. Need a new poncho because your current one looks like a kitchen colander? You'll have more luck patching the one you have than getting a replacement from the supply sergeant. Going to the field and need an ISO mat? Provo very likely would bark "I don't have any more ISO mats. This isn't a Walmart you know. And stop being a p...y about sleeping on the ground."

Despite his irritable and desultory demeanor, the man showed up for chapel service with unflinching regularity. Every Sunday he arrived at a quarter till the hour, sat in the same seat, and remained resolutely silent throughout the service. He never spoke to the other parishioners, never joined in singing hymns, and never said so much as a goodbye when leaving.

One of the few people that had kind words for Provo was Chaplain Gilmore. He appreciated that despite the sergeant having been cross leveled into the unit only five days before they deployed, he had managed to rapidly get up to speed. That was no accident. The man was a hard worker and he knew his business.

The regular supply sergeant (an affable middle-aged fellow named Brewer) had been injured during HEAT training. When extracting himself from a Humvee that had been turned upside down panic set in. Forgetting to brace himself with one hand on the roof of the vehicle (which had, for all intents and purposes, become the floor), he released his seatbelt. The sergeant's descent earthward was spectacular. As was the sound of his Kevlar clad head hitting metal.

A trip to the ER revealed several bulging disks. The doctors gave him orders for rest, rehab, and as a bonus suggested he lose some weight. Upon returning that night to the unit everyone agreed he looked reasonably

. . . .

relaxed in his shiny new neck brace. This level of composure, however, was most likely due to Demerol rather than a sanguine view if his good fortune. But none of that mattered. Nothing at this point would make him deployable. Consequently, three days later SGT Provo reported to the unit as the Supply Sergeant replacement. Five days after that the unit was wheels up heading for Afghanistan.

It was five months into the deployment when SGT Provo took his mid-tour leave. He was absent for almost a month: the time to transit out of and back into theater added nearly two weeks to the normal two week leave. When he returned to base Provo's normally dysphoric mood appeared even gloomier than usual. What's more, he had not been seen in chapel since returning from leave.

This happened with many soldiers. Chaplain Gilmore had come to expect that some of those in his flock would simply come and go. He tried to walk a fine line between following up on their lack of attendance in order to be an encourager, and knowing when to let things slide in order not to be seen as a nagging pastor.

Given Provo's perpetually grumpy demeanor, he concluded that pursuing his attendance at chapel would be viewed as harassment. With a slightly guilty sense of relief, he let the matter rest.

Several more weeks passed when on a Sunday evening there was a loud rapping on the door of Gilmore's CHU. Upon opening the door the chaplain found SGT Murray, the CHU mate of SGT Provo. After apologizing for coming by so late in the evening Murray asked if the chaplain had a minute to speak privately.

"Of course" Gilmore answered, hoping his hesitancy did not show. It had been a long day and he was looking forward to having a couple hours by himself. He thought "Even Jesus let the disciples struggle in the storm while he stayed on the hillside. Would it be so wrong to send this young man away until the morning?" His conscience prevailed, and he invited the sergeant into his CHU.

Taking a seat in a folding chair next to the chaplain's bunk SGT Murray *rubbed his hands together briskly before speaking. "Chaplain, I need your help. You know SGT Provo?"*

The question seemed rhetorical inasmuch as the chaplain knew all the soldiers in his unit. "I think he's not right. I mean, I think he's gone over the edge. He's acting like a crazy mother f--... Sorry sir, he's acting crazy."

Chaplain Gilmore's silence was enough to encourage the sergeant to continue. Murray went on to explain that when his shift finished earlier that night, and he returned to his CHU, Provo was sitting on the edge of his rack talking to himself.

"At first I didn't think much of it sir. I mean hell, maybe he just needed some alone time, right? So I just grabbed my gear and headed off to the chow hall. But when I came back he was still sitting there, kind of like he never moved... but now the son of a bitch had an M16 in his hands."

The sergeant went on to say that there was no magazine in the weapon but Provo continued to rack the weapon, the pull the trigger, and repeat the process over and over again.

Provo ignored Murray when he asked what was going on. After watching this routine for several minutes SGT Murray decided that sleep was out of the question, and a little help from the chaplain was needed. "So that's why I'm here Chaplain. It's weird. I really think he's lost it."

Chaplain Gilmore paused to think. He would really have preferred that Combat Stress Control be involved, but having them knock on Provo's door late at night seemed unlikely to be well received.

The chaplain quickly formulated a plan. He would take Murray with him to the TOC, inform the acting commander of the situation, and request a couple of escorts to stand outside Provo's CHU while he went in to talk with the sergeant. In all probability this was something that could be resolved with a little patience and support. But if not, he didn't like the idea of being with a distressed soldier who was comforting himself by playing with an M16.

Upon arriving at Provo's CHU he had the escorts stand far aside of the door so they would not be seen. No sense in alarming the sergeant. He then knocked, waited a half minute and knocked again. Nothing. "SGT Provo. This is Chaplain Gilmore. Mind if I talk with you for a bit?"

A moment later the door opened and Provo's grim face could be seen backlit by the florescent lights of the CHU. "Hey, Chaplain. You're out sort of late aren't you? Did you run out of Bibles? Need an emergency order?" His attempt at humor seemed more belligerent than friendly.

Ignoring the tone Gilmore responded, "I keep all sorts of hours. I heard that you were a little tense so I thought I would just drop by. Can we talk?"

"A little tense?" SGT Provo responded with a smirk. "Wonder who would have told you that." Not getting a response, the supply sergeant shrugged his shoulders. "Sure. Come on in but I've got to get some sleep soon. My day starts early." Upon entering the CHU Gilmore saw that the sergeant's M16 was still laying on his bunk. A magazine was placed next to it. Noticing the chaplain's gaze SGT Provo exclaimed "Oh, yeah, I was cleaning my weapon."

"Is that all?" the chaplain responded.

"Well, that and a function check. If those Taliban come through the wire I want to be ready" Provo said with a strained laugh.

The chaplain decided to get to the point. "SGT Murray came to me tonight. He's concerned...And so am I. Maybe we can take a few minutes to talk about what's going on. Seems like you're under a lot of stress."

Provo looked at the chaplain without expression. "Under stress you think? Hmmm. Let me see. I go on leave and learn that my girlfriend has been cheating on me, my son doesn't want to talk with me, and my ex-wife is moving to another state and filed court papers to take my boy with her. In the meantime, I get to come back to this little piece of paradise for another six months and let everything I've worked for back home go down the toilet. Yeah, I'm a little pissed. I don't know if that's stressed, but if you say so fine."

Although the particulars of Provo's story were unique, the theme of life turned inside out during a mid-tour leave was all too familiar. Gilmore had heard this tale of frustration and heart ache many times.

Every soldier responds differently to the stress of deployment when things on the home front fall apart. Getting angry, depressed, and feeling helpless were pretty common. Repetitively racking an M16 while sitting in your CHU was not. This was different and the chaplain needed to find out more about what Provo was thinking.

"That sounds awful. I'm sorry to hear that... maybe we can get legal involved and see what can be done to keep your ex-wife from moving your boy. That would be a start."

SGT Provo looked at the chaplain and sneered. "Is legal going to get my girlfriend to stop sleeping around as well? Are they going to get a court order to make my son want to talk with me?"

"What I'm saying is going to legal would be a start," the chaplain replied. "We can find some other ways to work on helping you deal with the breakup of your relationship, and how to re-connect with your son. It won't be easy, but I've seen other soldiers who have done it. Right now let's just take things one step at a time."

"Not an option. No offense but not interested chaplain."

"So what is your plan? Just tough it out for the remainder of the deployment? That sounds like a rough road to go down. I would love to help you out... if you'll let me," Gilmore responded.

"No. I'm not going to just tough it out. I'm working on a plan. Don't have all the details figured out just yet but there are ways to make my worthless ex-wife pay, and get back at Darlene."

"Darlene. That's your girlfriend?"

"You don't miss a step, do you, sir?" the supply sergeant shot back.

Chaplain Gilmore had worked with many soldiers who were agitated, angry, or in some way at the end of their rope. But Provo's unvarnished disdain and lack of military bearing was striking. It was tempting to shift his approach away from that which was consistent with the cross he wore on the collar of his ACUs and instead emphasize the captain bars that were clearly visible on his chest. Provo was beginning to irritate him, and for a moment he considered the value of giving the supply sergeant a good old-fashioned kick in the backside. Instead he reminded himself that the bigger mission on this evening was to look after the safety of his soldiers, including Provo, and those that Provo might hurt if he were as mentally unstable as the chaplain feared.

"Payback time?" the chaplain commented.

"That's right. Teach those whores a lesson." Chaplain Gilmore did not like the direction this was going, particularly the increasing anger that the specialist was showing. He had seen enough young soldiers in distress to know very well that when they became angry, and bent on revenge, rational thought pretty much went out the window. The two sat in silence for a minute.

Gilmore eventually spoke, carefully striking a matter of fact tone. "Tell me about your son. You said he isn't speaking to you. How were things before you deployed?"

"OK, yeah, they were OK. Not great. Not like they were before the divorce. But getting a little better" Provo responded. "He's just a little kid, you know. What does an eight-year-old know when his parents split up? So he kind of shut down when that happened, and I think his mom sort of screwed him up talking all kinds of crap about me. Before all of that we were close. He was my little buddy."

"Got any pictures?" the chaplain asked. SGT Provo looked surprised, and stared back at the chaplain without answering. "Of your son, Provo" the Gilmore clarified.

Provo pulled out his phone and after a moment of fiddling with the settings handed it to the chaplain. There were dozens of photos of a young boy who had a striking resemblance to the young man sitting in front of the chaplain. After asking a few questions about the photos Gilmore could see that Provo was starting to relax a little. Time to try and engage him again to see what he meant by getting revenge. He already had a pretty good idea but needed to be sure.

"Listen sergeant, you mentioned something about teaching your ex-wife, and your girlfriend, a lesson. What do you have in mind?" Provo stared at Gilmore wondering if he could be trusted. After a moment he laughed "Hell, why not?", and began to describe his plans.

"You see, I've been thinking it over. Noodling it through you know? And the thing I've come to realize... what would cause these two snakes the most pain is if I were killed in combat. Problem is, I work in supply! More likely to die of a heart attack than ever go outside the wire and die in combat."

"Glad to hear you're going to be with us for the duration" Gilmore said with relief. "Not so fast chaplain. There are other ways to skin this cat. Like taking matters into my own hands. Chamber a round, point, then pull the trigger. Other guys have done it... I mean why not join those few proud men that just said 'F... it?"

" You sound pretty determined" Gilmore reflected.
" You could say that," Provo responded tersely, the tension once more back in his voice.

"And what about your boy?" the chaplain asked. "Is he a part of this plan to get back at your wife and girlfriend? Because it sure sounds like he is going to get the same payback that everyone else gets?"

Provo looked pained and Gilmore knew he had hit a nerve. "He gets to grow up without a dad, and he gets to live his whole life knowing that you decided to blow your brains out rather than come back home to him. Oh, and he also gets to live the rest of his life not having mended his relationship with you after the divorce. That's a pretty heavy price for an eight-year old to pay so his dad can get revenge."

Provo stood up quickly and angrily said "Are you saying I'm a lousy dad? Is that your idea of helping? You sound like my wife. You--"

Gilmore broke in. "Hold on sergeant. That's not what I said." The chaplain's voice was harsher than he intended... he didn't care. Taking a deep breath before continuing, Gilmore added " You've misunderstood me. What I'm trying to get across is that you've not thought this through. You've not considered how this would hurt your son."

Provo stood and began to nervously pace while rubbing his face. "Have a seat. You need to focus for a minute so we can solve this thing."

The sergeant obeyed and began to say something but the chaplain ignored him. "All I've said is that your son will pay a very high price if you get revenge by killing yourself. From what you've told me about how much he means to you, I suspect that this would be the last thing in the world you want. What good is revenge if it ends up killing a part of your little boy's life? You know it would haunt him. I just don't think you've given it enough thought."

The sergeant's shoulders sagged under the weight of that last comment, and his eyes became moist. "Listen, what I said before is worth thinking about. Let's get legal involved. They can slow down this whole moving out of state business that your ex-wife has in mind. Then let me talk with command and see if you can join the ADVON party which would get you back to your son at least a month earlier."

Provo was silent, now sitting on the edge of his rack, head bowed in thought as his hands ran back and forth over his knees. " You've got nothing to lose," Gilmore continued ,"and your son has everything to gain."

After several more minutes of talking, Provo agreed to the chaplain's plan. He also agreed to accompany Gilmore on a visit to the Combat Stress Control clinic. If they were lucky, the psychiatrist might still be on duty and willing to prescribe something to help take the edge off.

They stepped out of the CHU and into the hot desert air. Provo looked at the guards standing next to his door. "Really?" he sneered. Without replying the chaplain began walking toward the clinic.

A short time later, as Gilmore was leaving Provo with a clinic social worker, he tried to provide some reassurance. "Sergeant, I know things look tough right now, but hang in there and you'll get through it. In fact, drop by my office tomorrow and we can talk for a bit longer."

Provo glanced up at the chaplain and said "Uh, thanks anyway, Chaplain. I think I've got this now. If you'll talk to the commander that's all I need. Going by your office sounds like something that will lead to a bunch of religious talk or praying. So thanks but no thanks."

The chaplain looked perplexed. "A guy who goes to church as often as you do is afraid of a little prayer?"

Provo laughed, and again shot a contemptuous look at Gilmore. " Yeah, I never miss a service. The command has to let me attend religious services. It's my right. Two hours off every Sunday where I don't have to be anybody's supply bitch." The chaplain's patience was wearing thin. Turning to leave, he replied evenly, "Good luck sergeant."

As Gilmore walked back to his CHU he reflected that his work as a chaplain was a mixed blessing. He was glad he had gotten to step in and help Provo out before the sergeant did something tragic. On the other hand, he couldn't stop thinking that he understood why the ex-wife would have a hard time working anything out with a man like Provo.

The sergeant never stepped foot back into supply. He spent that night at the CSC and the next morning the psychiatrist sent a recommendation to command for Provo to be removed from theater. Immediately. The sergeant's potential for suicide was too high to have him operate independently on base. As the commander was not one to assign battle buddies in these situations, he wasted no time drafting the necessary order. From his perspective, it would be bad for morale to keep Provo in the unit. The sooner he left the better. Within 48 hours the sergeant and his escort were on a plane headed to the States.

Identifying And Responding to Suicide Risk

The incidence of suicide and attempted suicide is a major concern within the military. This concern is well founded. In 2012 the suicide rate per 100,000 military personnel was 22.7. Significantly higher than the general population (approximately 18 per 100,000). The good news is that with the recent decreased operational tempo the incident rate of suicide in the military has decreased to 18.7 per 100,000 (as of 2015). Again, approximately the same as for the civilian population when adjusted for age and other demographics. It is of note, however, that the rate varies per service. For example, the rate per 100,000 is 23 for the Army, 23.1 for the Marine Corps, 14.4 for the Air Force and 13.4 for the Navy.[7]

Moreover, it appears that the stressors placed on reservists/ guard members may make them even more susceptible to suicidality when compared to the active component of the military. In 2013, the rate among reservists was 23.4 per 100,000, and among National Guardsmen, 28.9 per 100,000 (compare these to the 22.7 rate for active military during that time).

What accounts for the rise in suicide during the ten years bracketed from 2003 to 2013? Many researchers have come to the common-sense conclusion that the increase was due to the higher operational tempo during that time. Others, however, have suggested that the rise in suicide was due to the military having more lax standards for admission (due to the need for more recruits).

Whatever the explanation, as a chaplain in the military you can be certain that suicidality will be a problem with which you will be called upon to provide help (even during times of peace). Soldiers will come to you in great distress, sometimes facing the most demanding situations of their lives, and you will need to discern when that distress has reached a point wherein the soldier is at risk of taking his life. The challenge is demanding, and the research to date that focuses on effectively identifying suicidality reflects just how difficult it is to make an accurate assessment of risk and then effectively intervene.[8]

Fortunately there are some clear guidelines that will help you make informed decisions about a soldier's level of risk and then be able to act accordingly. These guidelines are simple, straightforward, and used by most therapists. Moreover, they are entirely consistent with

---

7   http://www.militarytimes.com/story/military/pentagon/2015/01/16/
    defense-department-suicides-2013-report/21865977/

8   (http://www.healthquality.va.gov/guidelines/MH/
    srb/VADODCP_SuicideRisk_Full.pdf).

ACE (Ask, Care and Escort), the standard approach recommended by the Army.

Initial Engagement

When an individual refuses to be candid about their state of mind, and their intentions, that it becomes very difficult to render appropriate help. If you were to ask most experienced therapists about suicidal patients they would tell you that there is little you can do if someone is thoroughly committed to ending their life. The person who has come to that decision, and made a commitment to act on their goal, is unlikely to provide you with much information. Their concern, of course, is that you will intervene and thwart their plans if they reveal their true intentions. It is in light of this understanding that it becomes extremely important to identify suicidal tendencies before they become entrenched and the individual becomes committed to the goal of killing himself.

Although it may be that it is not possible to identify the individuals who are absolutely intent on hiding their suicidal plans, it is possible to engage the majority of people who are contemplating suicide, and in so doing change the course of their lives. For these situations certain interviewing guidelines will prove immensely helpful. In the following section we will review these guidelines: you will find them simple and straightforward. Moreover, they are used by nearly all therapists when talking to someone wherein there are concerns about suicidality.

Many chaplain's wonder when they should ask about suicidal thoughts with someone they are counseling. Chaplain's also ask whether making such an inquiry runs the risk of prompting the person to begin thinking about suicide when they otherwise would not do so. Another common question is how does one go about tactfully asking about such thoughts. These are good questions, and each can be answered simply.

Whenever you are working with someone who is extremely distressed raise the question about suicidal thoughts. It is much better to err on the side of caution than to overlook something with such devastating consequences. Even if the soldier does not appear to be extremely distressed, yet his comments cause you to wonder whether he may be contemplating suicide, it is a good idea to raise the issue.

How to do so? Although tact is important, it is even more important to be direct. If you can combine tact and candor all the better. One easy way to accomplish this is to phrase your question along the following lines "You've told me about a number of things that are clearly troubling you, which is understandable. Have you ever gotten to the point where the stress of all of this has led you to think about hurting yourself?" If the soldier responds "yes" then you move on to conduct a suicide assessment. On the other hand, if the soldier responds "no" I would encourage you to press a little further, this time more specifically raising the issue of suicide. The follow up question could be phrased "So even though you have struggled with (insert the soldier's concerns), it has not crossed your mind to hurt yourself, or to end your life?" If the soldier responds with a long pause then this too will lead you to make further inquiries such as "I notice you really had to think about that answer. I'm wondering if perhaps these thoughts have crossed your mind. You certainly wouldn't be the first person I've spoken to who had such thoughts." Then see what response you get and go from there. Most of the time, however, if a person answers "no" to the first question, they will answer "no" to your follow up questions. Nevertheless it is worth your time to be thorough.

Will asking about suicide prompt suicidal thoughts? The answer is an emphatic "No." For those who are not suicidal the mention of suicide will not suddenly seem more attractive simply because you made an inquiry about the topic. For those who are contemplating suicide you will find that they frequently feel a great sense of relief in being able to tell someone what they have been keeping to themselves. Quite frequently when those who are thinking of ending their life feel a degree of shame or embarrassment. "I'm just weak" or "I'm such a failure to even have these thoughts" are common. Being able to share with someone else that such thoughts have crossed their mind is often quite reassuring.

Course of Suicide Risk

The majority of those who are at risk for suicide do not go on to complete the act of taking their own life. Nevertheless, the outcome for those that do move on to complete the act is so severe that it is best for the chaplain to err on the side of caution in making a thorough assessment and doing whatever is necessary to safeguard the soldier's well-being.

The outcome for those who do not attempt to end their lives is so variable that it is impossible to describe a general course of development and outcome for this mental health crisis. Many soldiers will resolve the stress that led them to this point and go on to lead full and happy lives. Others will experience a lifetime of psychological distress and periodically entertain the idea of ending their livesagain, only to stop short at the last moment. Still others, tragically, will resolve the momentary crisis that brought them to you only to re-experience overwhelming stress in the future that leads them to complete the act of suicide.

Assessment of Suicide Risk

There are many ways to assess for suicidality, but within each approach there lies some core elements. These include:

- Does the person have the intent to kill himself?
- Is there a plan with regard to how the person would kill himself?
- Does the person have the means for carrying out this plan, and is the plan lethal?

- Is the person willing to make a contract to contact you if he comes to the point wherein he feels that he will act on this plan?

Let's take a moment and discuss each of these elements in turn. The first, having to do with intent, must be approached by simply asking whether the soldier intends to act on the urge to commit suicide. The answer is seldom a straightforward "yes", but rather a "no" or "not really." You must inquire further in order to better assess how strongly the soldier is committed to ending his life.

One way to approach this is to ask "On a scale of one to ten, with one being no intention to kill myself and ten being absolutely committed to killing myself where would you rate yourself right now?" You should follow up with another question along the lines of "Using that same rating what is the highest you have been at?" Then ask for more information as to when this was, the specific circumstances, and what kept him from acting on the urge. It is a good idea to express your happiness that he did not act on the urge, and point out that he found ways to combat these self-destructive impulses. If he could do that once, he can do so again. Of course you can also use the same scale to ask "During the course of most days, where would you rate yourself on this scale?"

Asking about the suicide plan is just as straightforward. For instance, you might comment "You've told me that you've had suicidal thoughts. Even though you have also said that you don't think you would act on them I would like to talk about this for a little bit if you don't mind. When you've contemplated ending your life, in what way have you thought about doing so?" From there find out the specifics. If the soldier tells you he has thought of shooting himself you will want to know with what gun? Where? When?

The answers you receive will naturally open up other lines of inquiry. If the soldier appears to grow frustrated by your questions simply reassure him that you only want to make certain that you thoroughly understand him, and in that way can be of most help. During the course of this questioning you will also be able to determine the lethality of the plan. A soldier who plans to shoot himself (especially when he has access to a firearm) has a more lethal plan than one who plans to starve himself. Obviously, the former plan will in turn cause you to be more concerned.

Other considerations must also be made when assessing for suicidality. You will want to know whether the soldier has recently gone through a particularly troubling experience. Particularly an experience that leaves him feeling guilty, ashamed, or hopeless. Divorce, legal issues, death of a loved one, losing rank, etc. are just a few of the many examples you will come across. One should also look for depression, social withdrawal, drastic changes in behavior, an obsession with death, and giving away possessions. No one characteristic will be indicative of a high risk for suicide, but each of these can be used as signposts suggesting a need on your part to be more cautious about the soldier's risk for self-harm.

At this point you have completed the suicide assessment. You are satisfied that you have sufficient information about the soldier's suicide risk. Now you are faced with a decision. Should the soldier be hospitalized (generally reserved for soldiers who have a clear and lethal plan and express a high intent to take their life), or do you develop a 'no harm' contract with the soldier. With the clear Army policy noting that a soldier's communication to a chaplain be kept strictly confidential, your ability to move a soldier towards hospitalization is limited. It is, in these instances, a matter of persuasion. Easier, however, is gaining the soldier's support for entering into a 'no harm' contract. Although this does not provide an iron clad guarantee that the soldier will not attempt suicide, in many situations it is the best that can be done.

Key Symptom Checklist For Suicide Risk

Is the soldier distressed (e.g., depressed, showing extreme guilt/ embarrassment, hopelessness, anger, etc.)?

Have there been major disruptions in the soldier's life leading up to this distress (e.g., divorce, death of a loved one or close friend, demotion, loss of job opportunities, onset of major illness, etc.)?

Does the soldier express an intent, even if mixed with ambivalence, to end his life?

Does he have a plan, and if so is it a specific plan for ending his life?

Is the plan lethal?

Does the soldier have the means to carry out the plan?

Is the soldier unable to identify personally compelling reasons for not taking his life?

Is there a history of past suicide attempts?

Is there a history of impulsively acting out?

The risk of suicide is greater as more of these questions are answered in the affirmative.

Chaplain Interventions for Suicide Risk

Now that you have assessed the soldier and found that he is at risk for self-harm, the question is how to reduce and eventually resolve this threat. If the soldier has agreed to go to mental health, then your role *may* in his care may be complete, and the following is not relevant. But there is a very real possibility that the soldier will wish to continue to see you, whether he has agreed to mental health services or not. If he is being seen by a therapist I would strongly recommend that you coordinate your pastoral counseling effortswith those offered by the therapist. If the soldier is not being seenby a therapist, but continues to see you, then it will be up to you to formulate a plan by which to reduce the threat of suicide.

Many counselors approach the task of intervening with suicidal clients by focusing on the diagnosis that has been given to the person. The idea being if the symptoms can be reduced then the threat of self-harm will likewise be ameliorated. There is no denying the logicin this plan. Unfortunately reducing symptoms is often not sufficientin order to effectively change the threat of suicide. Other factors also play an important role in mediating risk. This includes the soldier's ability to *problem solve* issues of personal concern, intense *emotional dysregulation*, a *lack of reasons for living*, believing that they are a *burden on others*, a *sense of shame/guilt*.

To be most effective in helping the soldier you will need to identify which of these dynamics (or others) are at work, and find ways to help remediate those issues you have identified. Fortunately, chaplains are very familiar with helping individuals who feel a sense of shame or guilt, and those that see little purpose in life. What chaplains wrestle with more often is how to implement practical interventions for helping people to become better problem solvers and gain control over their emotions. This is what we will look at next. If a person can begin to feel confident that the problems with which they are faced are also problems with which they are prepared to resolve, hope takes root. Moreover, once a person begins to gain control over their emotions then balance begins to be established. Both these elements, hope and balance, are essential companions along the road leading back from precipice of suicide.

Inasmuch as we already discussed the 'No Harm' contract in the previous section of this chapter, we will not review it again here. It is enough to note that it is a frequent part of any intervention plan with suicidal ideation.

Problem Solving

With regard to problem solving there are many approaches one could take, but the simplest (yet effective) means for helping increase this capacity is to first identify the problem for the soldier, and then teach a simple four step process. It is beyond the scope of this manual to go into great detail here, but the process is sufficiently straightforward that a brief outline is likely to suffice.

Step 1: Identify the problematic
Step 2: Brain storm possible solutions
Step 3: Select what appears to be the best solution
Step 4: Employ that solution
Step 5: Assess results and if need be return to Step One.

When teaching these steps it is best to write them down (those who are distressed have a tendency to easily forget). Have the soldier select a problem that they currently are facing, or recently encountered. Go through the process with the soldier being sure to note any steps that are particularly difficult for him to complete (be sure to spend extra time reviewing those steps).

It is worth noting that often times a distressed individual will unwittingly exaggerate the consequences of selecting an imperfect solution to the problems he faces. Be mindful of this and specifically ask what may happen if the solution they employ is not successful. If the response is realistic all the better, but if it is overly catastrophic then take time to question this assumption, and bring the personback to a more realistic view of the situation.

It is also worth noting that effective problem solving is significantly hampered when someone has poor control over their emotions. Therapists refer to this as 'emotional dysregulation.' Ifthe soldier you are helping shows signs of having this difficulty it will require you to provide some assistance. Again, there are many approaches to helping in this regard, more than can be examined here, but a couple of common means for teaching better emotional control are worth our attention. The first of these involves learning to calm oneself in the moment.

Focused Breathing

For many years therapists have known that one of the most immediate ways to induce a more calm/relaxed state of mind is to engage in slow, focused, diaphragmatic breathing (Varvogli & Darvir, 2011).

Distress frequently disrupts the normal breathing pattern. Most often this results in the individual taking shorter more rapid breaths, sometimes to the point of hyperventilation. This change in breathing pattern in turn leads to greater tension. What you wish to help the distressed soldier learn is to recognize when he is beginning to feel distressed, and then make a conscious effort to alter his breathing into one that resembles the pattern typical of a person who is calm. The impact is often immediate. Although it is unlikely to entirely eliminate the distress, it goes a long way toward restoring a sense of balance and clarity of thought.

The steps for teaching this skill are straightforward.

- Provide a rationale (per the description above)
- Have the soldier sit relaxed in a chair or on a couch
- Demonstrate for the soldier how to take a deep breath using one's diaphragmatic muscles (see explanation below)
- Count slowly to three as you inhale and then slowly to three as you exhale (do not hold your breath at either the top of the inhalation or exhalation)
- Now have the soldier breath in the same fashion as you continue to model the same

It can be very helpful to add to one or two elements to the breathing exercise, although it is by no means required. The first of these is to have the soldier imagine with each inhalation that he is breathing in "clean, refreshing, calming air" deep into his lungs and it is then flowing throughout his body. Sometimes having the person imagine a particular color for this calming air is also helpful. Likewise, have the soldier imagine that during each exhalation he is breathing out the stress. Again, having a color or some other concrete quality associated with the exhalation of the "stressful breath" can make this more effective.

The other element that is often added to this exercise is to have the individual, after taking several deep breaths, to remain relaxed in the chair for a few moments. During this time have them notice the stress that remains in their shoulders and then tell them to allow their shoulders to lower some, to feel warmth slowly seeping into their shoulder muscles, and to allow the tension in those muscles to escape. Take a pause, and a few moments later tell the soldier that he can then allow this same relaxing warmth to spread down to his arms and feel the tension evaporating in these muscles as well.

You may want to comment that they can just let their arms sink down on the chair (their lap, or where ever they have placed their arms). Then finally mention their hands: that they can relax their hands and feel the tension flowing out of their palms and fingers. Finish this by having them take one or more deep breaths, again inhaling the "relaxing, fresh, clean air" and exhaling any remaining tension while clearing their mind of worries.

Most people who go through this protocol experience noticeable relief after one attempt. You should ask if the soldier whether he feels less stressed at this point. Although it is unlikely that this simple exercise will have relieved all stress, you will normally find that it has relieved at least some of the stress. At this point you let him know that like any skill it will become stronger, and more effective, with practice. With that in mind the soldier should be encouraged to practice going through this exercise at least once and preferably twice a day (each practice session should last at least five minutes).

Before ending this section, I want to mention one more powerful way you may wish to intervene with suicidal soldiers. Demonstrate that you care. Research shows that patients who receive a follow up message or telephone call from their intake therapist (to whom they had been assigned due to suicidal ideation) are much less likely to harm themselves when compared to patients who had not received any follow up. Ongoing messages/calls are all the better. For the soldier contemplating suicide, it can be a profoundly moving experience to realize that the chaplain believes they are important enough to be remembered later in the week. Such interest and compassion are never wasted, and in these instances can be genuinely lifesaving.

Summary Of Chaplain Interventions for Suicide Risk

Develop a 'No Harm' contract
Confront the soldier's sense of guilt/shame/lack of purpose
Teach practical problem-solving skills
Teach relaxation techniques (to reduce affective dysregulation)
Frequent follow up contact until crisis is resolved, then taper
   accordingly

PANIC ATTACK DISORDER

*L*TC Alan Berkshire came from a long line of military men. His father had fought in the Battle of Bulge, and his grandfather had fought with the 2nd Battalion, 5th Marines in WWI at the Battle of Belleau Wood. Prior to this, previous generations in his family had fought in the Spanish American War, Civil War and the Revolutionary War. It was a tradition his family was rightfully proud of, and as a matter of course it was expected that he too would step forward to serve in the military in some capacity when he reached adulthood.

Alan had relished the challenge of meeting this expectation and had enlisted in the Army the day after graduating from high school. After serving four years in the 2nd Armored Division he discharged from active duty and entered college in the late 1980s.

Upon completing a degree in economics from Bowling Green University Alan went on to open his own business. He also entered the Army Reserves and received a commission as an officer in the Army Reserves. As he told his friends, the Army was something that he just couldn't get out of his system. Eventually he transferred into the 55th Sustainment Brigade. It was with this unit that he entered Iraq in March 2008, stationed at Joint Base Balad.

Although LTC Berkshire had eagerly looked forward to the deployment, he also had misgivings. Would his family be hurt by his prolonged absence? Would his business survive during his absence? How much real danger would he face? These concerns embarrassed him, and he felt it best to keep these worries to himself. Push them out of sight.

"After all" he reasoned "Once I'm in theater I will be much too busy to worry about anything except the mission. No sense making a big deal about this stuff, after all, no one else does."

Unfortunately, like so many deployments, this one had come at a bad time. Berkshire's wife was unhappy that she would be left on her own for an entire year. She had often complained of feeling like a single parent. His business, and the Reserves, left little time for family. He fretted and often lay awake at night wondering if the stress of a deployment would crush his already fragile marriage?

Just as disconcerting was the fear that his private practice as a financial planner would be devastated by a yearlong absence. Although colleagues had volunteered to work with his clients while he was away, Berkshire knew what would happen. Many of his customers would never return. What then? And how big would the loss be? Would he need to start rebuilding the business all over again?

It was a relief when these concerns receded during the weeks of premobilization training. He was kept busy, morale was high, and the unit was hitting all of its pre-mob objectives. It had been a long time since he felt this excited about soldiering.

But after arriving in Iraq, going through the transfer of command, and settling into the rhythm of a daily work routine, the worries returned. His initial excitement had faded, and anxiety rushed in to fill the void.

Berkshire tried to escape by going to the gym, visiting the USO, and working late. Anything that offered a distraction. But nothing worked. The fears hung on like fish hooks, piercing every waking hour of the day.

He sometimes looked at other soldiers who appeared not to have a care in the world and wondered how they managed. What was their secret? *"Maybe the only secret"* he mused *"Is that I'm not cut out for being deployed"*

Like a movie reel that plays on an endless loop, worse case scenarios darted across the screen of his mind. Returning from deployment to an empty *home, a depleted bank account, and a failed business. With these worries came a lack of sleep, which over time began to impact Berkshire's ability to concentrate. Not infrequently he began to forget important details about assignments and missions. In briefings he would silently fight down panic when the Commander reminded everyone that "The success of sustainment hinges on nailing 100 percent of the details 100 percent of the time."*

Thus far he had been lucky. When he had overlooked some aspect of a task his assistant, a young captain, had caught the mistake and tactfully brought it to his attention. But he couldn't count on his luck holding out over another seven months of deployment. What would happen if he were in a meeting with his commander and committed that type of error?The thought terrified him. He liked his commander. Respected her, and thought her to be a reasonable leader. But he also knew that Commander Riechert had little tolerance for someone who was not up to the job. During pre-deployment he had seen the commander dismiss a certain major from the deployment battle roster for having made the same mistake twice. Alan Berkshire could not afford to have his family's legacy smeared by his performing poorly in Iraq. He could never live that down, and the mere thought of it caused his heart to race.

Over the ensuing month things continued to deteriorate. What brought things to a head involved a convoy to an outlying FOB. The convoy was to leave at 0600, and Berkshire was to arrive at the meet up point at 0430. He had forgotten to write the time down but was convinced that the convoy was leaving at 0800. Arriving at 0630 he found it had already left. The sergeant in charge of convoys could not give him much information beyond the basics. Yes, the convoy had been scheduled to leave at 0600. No, the time had not been changed, and yes, his name had been on the travel roster. A cold fear gripped LTC Berkshire as his mind raced to find a reasonable explanation to give to his commander. None came to mind. There was nothing to do but go back and tell COL Reichert that he had missed the convoy.

The meeting with his commander did not go well. The colonel did not understand how anyone could miss getting on a convoy. Something was said along the lines of "This isn't astrophysics you know. It's simple, like finding your way back to your CHU at night. You can do that can't you? How can a guy from sustainment not be able to figure out the logistics of getting on an MRAP so he can travel to another base?"

It went on for some time, but LTC Berkshire felt fortunate that his commander was not the type to scream: then the entire shop would have had a front row seat to his humiliation. The commander finished by telling him, "If we were still in pre-mob I would pull you off the battle roster. But since we're already in theater it would be a pain in my butt to explain to the higher ups why I'm sending you home. That means you get one more chance. You get that, right? ONE more chance. You need to get your head straight Berkshire. Get your head in the game because we're here for another five months and I need you to be 100 percent. Am I being clear?"

Berkshire thought the commander could not be any clearer had she used a blackboard and markers to spell out her point. "Perfectly clear ma'am."

"In that case were done here."

LTC Berkshire hightailed it out of the TOC like a preacher leaving a prayer meeting: no eye contact and double speed. It was this haste that caused him to quite literally charge into Chaplain Mendoza as he left the building. Mendoza had seen LTC Berkshire often during their deployment but never at chapel services. Although they had exchanged pleasantries, and discussed in general terms how the unit was performing, Mendoza had little personal knowledge of the LTC. After nearly being knocked down, and dropping the box that he had been carrying, the chaplain regained his balance and clapped the LTC on the shoulder. "My friend, you seem to be charging into battle! But remember, I'm on your side." With that the chaplain let out a loud laugh. Typical of Chaplain Mendoza, he was his own best audience. It was part of his charm: funny, self-effacing, warm, and exuding the best qualities of his native Puerto Rico.

LTC Berkshire could not help but smile at the chaplain. Perhaps it was his recent humiliation, or Mendoza's winsome demeanor, but the LTC let his guard down a little. "I'm certainly not charging any enemies chaplain. More like a tactical retreat from a royal ass chewing."

Mendoza's demeanor became more serious as he paused to see if there was more the LTC wanted to say. Berkshire stood like an awkward schoolboy. He looked as though he wanted to say more, but could not make up his mind whether he should take the chance. The chaplain studied him closely and made a decision. "Hey, this is your lucky day my friend. You see this box? Inside are pieces of heaven, delivered by angels just this morning... or maybe in the mail." Berkshire looked puzzled and stared at the box under the chaplain's arm. "Polvorones!" Mendez whispered in a conspiratorial tone.

The LTC's expression remained blank. "Puerto Rican cookies" the chaplain explained with enthusiasm. "My wife bakes the best polvorones on the island. No, the best in the world. And I've tasted my share of polvorones. Even better than my mother... but if you ever meet my mother and tell her I said that I will call you a liar!" Once again there was the infectious Mendoza laugh. "I tell what my friend, let's go over to my office and have some of these cookies. I'll put on a pot of strong coffee. Come with me, please, you'll be my guest and for a moment we will pretend to be on the back porch of my home in Fajardo looking out over the ocean."

With that Chaplain Mendoza turned and began to quickly stride toward his office. LTC Berkshire felt it would be rude not follow him, and besides, the idea of escaping to the islands, even if only in his imagination, seemed preferable to answering the questions from his subordinates as to why he was still on base rather than on a convoy.

It took only a few minutes for Mendoza to get the coffee brewing. His office had been furnished by the previous chaplain with Iraqi furniture, rugs and lamps. Among this assortment of middle eastern décor was a photograph of the chaplain's family, prominently displayed on his desk. After handing the LTC a cup of coffee Mendoza opened the box of polvorones. Berkshire smiled seeing what delight the chaplain took in opening this gift from his wife, and it turned his thoughts to his own wife who was seldom home when he called back to the states. Even when she did pick up the phone the conversations were not pleasant – her anger at his having been deployed had only deepened since his departure.

"So tell me, how bad was this butt chewing? You look like you can still sit without too much pain" Mendoza said cheerily, breaking into Berkshire's desultory reflections. "Is it so bad that surgery will be required, or will a trip to medic be sufficient?"

"Oh, no, not that bad" Berkshire chuckled. "I'll get over it fast enough. You know the commander. She can be tough, but she doesn't hold grudges."

"I'm glad to hear that." Mendoza replied, then turning more serious. "But if you don't mind I would like to hear what happened. It might help for you to blow up some steam." Now it was Berkshire who smiled – Chaplain Mendoza was well known for mangling figures of speech. He remembered an earlier time when the chaplain had counseled a young soldier not to take a superior's rebuke to heart, but let it roll off him "like water off a duck's butt."

Maybe telling the chaplain about his problems wasn't a bad idea after all – he had no one else in the unit to whom he could confide, why not the chaplain? Not that he didn't have friends, but Berkshire felt that it was unbecoming to disclose too much about his frustrations and struggles with anyone who shared command, let alone with subordinates. With that in mind, and a growing sense of relief, he began to tell his story. It started with discussing the missed convoy, and went back in time from there to include his wife's reaction when first learning about his deployment. The chaplain was a good listener, attentive to nuance, quick to identify when something had been glossed over, and very understanding. By the time they had finished their talk the coffee and cookies were nearly gone.

LTC Berkshire had discussed his growing fears, racing heart, sudden sweats, sense of dread, and ended with the conclusion that he was proving himself a failure. " You know chaplain, it's embarrassing not to be able to get this under control. It's unbelievable to me that I'm cratering under pressure. After all, it's not like we are in the Battle of the Bulge."

Chaplain Mendoza sighed. "My friend, you are your own worst enemy. You give yourself no mercy. I do not hear an ounce of charity for yourself. And until you start to ease up on this.... what do I want to say... until you stop beating yourself up, then you cannot begin to feel better."

Berkshire tersely began to reply "Maybe, the thing you have to remember--" but Mendoza cut him off.

"No, no. I no need to remember anything. I want you to listen, please. It seems to me that the commander's butt chewing does not compare to what you do to yourself. You are chewing your butt more than she did!" With that the chaplain once again broke into a fit of laughter, finding the visual image of what he said much too funny to contain his amusement.

Berkshire also laughed, and after a moment concluded that the chaplain was onto something. Mendoza confided that, in his opinion, panic attacks were keeping the colonel from being effective. This caught Berkshire's attention. After reviewing a symptom checklist together there was little room to doubt the diagnosis, even if it was informal.

Mendoza suggested that the fastest way for the colonel to deal with this would be to see someone at Combat Stress Control. As expected Berkshire demurred, "I have a career to think about. Maybe not much of a career, but I still hope to make something of it. Having this on my record wouldn't be good. But maybe you can help, yes? I already feel better from just this brief tulk."

Mendoza leaned back in his chair and sighed. He would have much preferred that the LTC use Combat Stress Control. "Ahh, yes, I could probably be of some help. That's true. But I think we both know you might get even more help from working with a therapist."

Berkshire brushed away the chaplain's suggestion. "I'll make you a deal. If you help me, that is if you meet with me some more, and if it doesn't do any good, then I'll reconsider going to Combat Stress."

The chaplain thought for a moment. "That's fair. I'll do my best, but you also need to do your best." The colonel was relieved. In fact, he felt more hopeful than he had in many weeks. " You can count on it. Sounds like we got ourselves a deal" he happily replied.

They quickly settled on a time to continue their talk and Berkshire started for the door. "Oh, one more thing Chaplain. Since we are going to be meeting for a while, should I expect that you will be serving more polvorones?"

Identifying and Responding to Panic Attack Disorder

Occasionally you will have a soldier come to you that describes debilitating episodes of extreme anxiety that arise suddenly and persist for anywhere from ten minutes to a couple hours. The soldier will describe his experience as one in which his heart is pounding, perhaps some light headedness, sweating, dizziness, nausea, a fear of losing control and most often a foreboding sense of imminent danger. Not all of these symptoms necessarily occur, but the soldier with panic attacks will definitely endorse some of the somatic (physical) sensations just listed, as well as extreme anxiety and foreboding. During these times of distress he will find it difficult to carry out his duties, and very likely find it difficult to focus his attention on anything other than the sense of panic that has suddenly taken hold of him.

Research has not yet uncovered the cause of panic disorders although they are not uncommon among those suffering from PTSD. When this is the case one often finds that some event has triggered a memory that in turn triggers this response. Don't expect the soldier to necessarily recall what that trigger was, or for that matter recall the memory that was stimulated. These "triggers" often occur outside of conscious awareness, and one only comes to identify them after a good deal of detective work after the panic attack has passed. Although most people who struggle with panic attacks do not have PTSD, it is wise to initially look for this connection when dealing with military personnel. Of course, if it is found that the cause is PTSD then the proper response is to make sure that the soldier receives treatment for that disorder. But to be clear, panic attacks can occur with any individual, not just those who have been traumatized. Indeed, the majority of people who struggle with this disorder have no history of trauma.

Course of Panic Attack Disorder

In the general population approximately 23% of people will have this disorder at some time in their lives. Without intervention the person who has panic attacks is likely to continue to intermittently struggle with this form of anxiety. It is not unusual for panic attacks to gradually interfere with an individual's day to day functioning, slowly eroding their productivity and impairing relationships with both family and friends. Due to the extreme distress that marks panic attacks many people eventually become fearful of leaving the house or engaging in any number of activities that they would normally enjoy. Consequently they become more and more reclusive in order to maintain some sense of safety and predictability in their lives. In extreme cases they may become so withdrawn that their fear of going out in public keeps them virtually home bound. This is termed agoraphobia. Because so many people with panic attack also have a history of being generally anxious, the panic attacks tend to confirm their view of the world as a frightening and unpredictable place over which they have little control.

Assessing for Panic Attack Disorder

Panic attacks come in three varieties: unexpected, situationally bound, and situationally predisposed. The unexpected panic attack occurs without any recognized 'triggering' situation. The situationally bound panic attack has a clear trigger: this may be a particular situation or even particular thoughts. Examples of this include the loss of an important relationship, failure at work, isolation, or even an odor that reminds the person of some feared event. Situationally bound panic attacks are similar, the difference being that the trigger does not invariably lead to a panic attack. When assessing for panic attacks it is always a good idea to keep in mind that many of the symptoms are also brought on by various medical conditions (e.g., cardiac dysfunction, thyroid conditions, etc.). Consequently, having the soldier consult with a physician is typically a good idea when possible.

Your conversation with a soldier that you suspect is suffering from panic attacks will start no differently than the other assessments described thus far. But let us assume that during the course of that conversation you gather information that leads you to believe that the underlying issue may be anxiety, and panic attacks in particular. At this point it is wise to simply tell the soldier that you wish to focus a little more specifically on his anxiety for a moment, and would like him to answer a number of questions that you've found helpful to raise with others who likewise struggle with anxiety. At that point you simply ask if he has experienced any of the following (see list below). When the answer to any of these questions is 'yes', take a moment to find out when that symptom occurred, how long it lasted, when he first experienced it, and how frequently it continues to arise.

Below is a list of questions that are helpful to ask when assessing for Panic Attack Disorder.

- Have you ever experienced palpitations, pounding heart, or an accelerated heart rate that came on suddenly and without anything that would account for this change?
- Have you ever experienced a sudden unexplainable onset of sweating?
- Have you ever experienced trembling or shaking without there being a clear physical cause?
- Have you ever experienced a shortness of breath, or a sense that you were smothering and there was no clear physical cause?
- Have you ever had the sense that you were choking but could find no reason for this perception?
- Have you ever experienced unexplainable chest pain/ discomfort without physical exertion?

- How often do you become nauseous (a high frequency is telling)?
- Have you ever experienced a sudden unexplainable feelings of dizziness or light headedness?
- Do you have times when anxious of feeling as though things, at that moment, are not quite real?
- Do you have times when feeling anxious that you also fear losing control or "going crazy"?
- Have you ever experienced, without there being a present danger, an intense fear of dying?
- Have you ever experienced a sudden unexplainable numbness or tingling sensations?
- Do you have periods of anxiety when you have the urge to flee or escape, and have a sense of impending doom?
- Do you spend a great deal of time worrying about when another anxiety attack will occur? If so, how severe are these worries (rated on a scale of 1 to 10 with 1 being no worries and 10 being severely worried).
- Do you find yourself avoiding people, places or situations that may trigger another anxiety attack?

The goal of asking these questions is not to derive a psychiatric diagnosis. I've mentioned this earlier in the manual: we are not looking for the most precise diagnosis that fits the soldier's symptoms, but instead are looking to get a 'working diagnosis', that is to find a generally accurate descriptor of the soldier's problems for which they have come to you for help. If we can do that we will have succeeded. (As a side note, psychiatric diagnoses are often rather unreliable even when derived by a social worker, psychiatrist or psychologist).[9] At

---

9   Studies show that the accuracy of diagnoses for depression is about 60%, and for anxiety disorders a little lower at 46%. Getting a descriptor that is 'in the ball park' will work just fine. (http://www.ncbi.nlm.nih.gov/pmc/

this point you want to briefly review the responses to the first 13 questions. If the soldier responded "yes" to four or more it is very likely that he is having panic attacks.

The next question is how is the anxiety impacting the soldier? To answer this look to the last two questions from the foregoing list. If the answers to these last two questions indicates the soldier spends a significant amount of time worrying about the next anxiety attack, and that he is actively avoiding people, places or situations that provoke such anxiety, you can be certain that panic attacks are at least one of the issues that should be addressed.[10]

Other concerns may well warrant your attention as well. Depression, for example, is a very common co-occurring problem with many anxiety disorders.[11] This likely occurs because anxiety frequently leads a person to eventually feel constantly under siege, yet helpless to affect change. This becomes fertile soil in which to grow a depressive disorder.

In addition, anxiety sufferers will often dramatically change their lifestyle in order to cope with their fears (e.g., social isolation, self-medicating with alcohol, etc.). This can easily lead to a sense of missing out on life, and failing to meaningfully engage in one's full potential. This too makes the onset of depression more likely.

In the 'Intervention' section of this chapter we will review a variety of simple ways that you can make a profound impact on the soldier with panic attacks.

---

articles/PMC3068718/ Int J Health Sci (Qassim). 2008 Jan; 2(1): 35–38. PMCID: PMC3068718 Accuracy of Referring Psychiatric Diagnosis)

10 Many soldiers are reluctant to admit that they have persistent worries, and even more reticent about admitting that these anxieties have a significant impact on their lives. With this in mind you may need to do a considerable amount of reassuring and probing in order to get a candid responses.

11 Kalin, Ned H., (2020) The Critical Relationship Between Anxiety and Depression, American Journal of Psychiatry, https://ajp. psychiatryonline.org/doi/10.1176/appi.ajp.2020.20030305

Key Symptom Checklist for Panic Attack Disorder

- Accelerated heart rate/palpitations.
- Profuse sweating not associated with physical exertion.
- Trembling/shaking associated with anxiety.
- Shortness of breath and/or sense of smothering not associated with physical exertion
- Sense of choking.
- Chest pain/discomfort associated with tension/anxiety.
- Repeated periods of nausea unrelated to physical illness
- Dizzy/lightheadedness
- During periods of anxiety feeling as though 'things are not quite real'
- Fear of losing control or 'going crazy'
- Intense fear of dying without clear and present threat
- Numbness or tingling in any part of the body
- Anxiety accompanied by urge to flee or escape
- Spending a great deal of time/energy worried about when a panic attack will occur
- Avoiding people, places or situations in order to avoid anxiety

Chaplain Interventions for Panic Attack Disorder

There is good news for the individual who suffers with panic attacks: when properly treated they nearly always can be resolved. There are several common approaches for treating panic attack disorder. In no particular order of importance these include the use of medications (benzodiazepines such as Valium, Ativan, Klonopin, and Xanax, or antidepressants within the SSRI class such as Zoloft and Prozac which also diminish anxiety). Non-medical interventions are also popular and most often focus on cognitive behavioral therapy (CBT). Of course some practitioners prefer to combine these approaches hoping to achieve a superior result. When considering these two approaches it is good to put them in perspective. The impact of medication on reducing anxiety is much faster than using CBT. The drawback is that quite often, once the anxious individual stops taking medication, the anxiety returns. CBT on the other hand helps the anxious person *learn how* to be less anxious, and having learned these skills the person is independently able to manage future flare ups.

The CBT approach to dealing with anxiety is straightforward and can be easily employed by chaplains. Panic attacks (like other anxiety disorders) are most often dealt with by using one or more of the following, which we will briefly examine in turn:

Relaxation

Cognitive Restructuring

Exposure

Relaxation

One cannot be relaxed and anxious at the same time. The two states are polar opposites. Consequently, it is important to teach the anxious soldier how to relax (no, not with a beer and cigarette, or a day at the beach). "Diaphragmatic breathing" is very often used for this purpose (see Chaplain Interventions for Generalized Anxiety Disorder for more details).

Have the soldier sit comfortably and practice taking a slow deep breath. The idea is to breath in focusing on using his belly muscles. That is, tell the soldier to take a slow deep breath while thinking of a chord running the length of his stomach, and this chord is pulling on his lungs thereby bringing in fresh soothing and refreshing air.

Demonstrate the method for him. Yes, it may seem silly initially, but once you have tried it a couple of times, your hesitancy will fade. The soldier needs an example to understand what he is being asked to do. As you breath in using this method, you'll notice that your stomach rises slightly. This is a sign that you are using diaphragmatic breathing.

Now have the soldier follow along. Once he has shown that he can take a deep breath in this fashion ask him to imagine a peaceful scene. Any scene he likes as long as it is pleasant and peaceful. Have him imagine the sights, sounds, smells, textures and anything else about the scene that makes it more vivid. Have him settle into a chair, imagine the scene, then take a slow deep breath. As he does so tell him to likewise imagine that he is inhaling clean, refreshing, and relaxing air that fills his body from head to toe. As he exhales have him imagine that he is breathing out anxiety (he can provide a color, or some other visual cue to make it more salient to him). While doing this he is to imagine the peaceful scene he had previously identified.

Continue this exercise for three to five breaths. At the beginning of the exercise you should ask him to rate his anxiety on a scale of 1 to 10, with 1 being no anxiety and 10 being a panic attack. At the end of the breathing exercise have him give you his rating. It is almost always lower, often much lower. Use this change in anxiety to assure him that he has control over his anxiety. He now has a tool that can provide some control.

The more he practices using this tool, the more effective he will become in gaining control over his anxiety. Remind the soldier that this is no different that PT: the more he practices running, the better his PT times and the easier it is to run faster and longer. He needs to practice this breathing exercise five more times per day. If he responds that this is too much remind him that it takes less than three minutes to practice taking five deep relaxing breaths. You have asked him to take 15 minutes of the day to help gain control over his panic attacks. This is a reasonable request and there is not a soldier who comes to you that cannot put aside this time each day.

Cognitive Restructuring

This term refers to the process of helping individuals think about the stressors that give rise to panic attacks in a different way. By viewing things differently, the anxiety lessens. One of the problems that occurs with people who experience panic attacks is that small events take on dire proportions. For example, the woman who is late with an assignment for work then begins to think, "I am going to be fired, and once I am unemployed no one will want to hire me. My life will be ruined." Or the man whose wife is running thirty minutes late returning from an errand begins to think, "My spouse is certain to be cheating on me. She is late because she is seeing someone behind my back. I bet she is cheating with that loser Steve. I saw them talking at the party last month."

These thoughts begin to take on a life of their own, they gain momentum quickly, and lead one to physically feel the sensation of anxiety rapidly mounting. As these sensations build the person then becomes alarmed that a panic attack is imminent and this leads to even greater anxiety.

The goal of cognitive restructuring is three-fold. First, to have the individual identify those thoughts that go through his mind just prior to and during a panic attack. Often such thoughts are so automatic that they occur outside of one's awareness. It is not unusual to ask someone who struggles with panic attacks what gives rise to them only to hear, "I have no idea."

By having someone think carefully about what they were doing prior to a panic attack, and what was on their mind, these thoughts can be reconstructed. Having soldiers keep a thought diary wherein they jot down what they are thinking during these times is also helpful. An example of how this can provide insights is found in the case of a woman who had no idea what gave rise to her debilitating panic attacks. When closely questioned about the evening when her first panic attack occurred, however, she recalled removing finger nail polish with a strong solvent. As she was doing so she thought, "I wonder if this stuff is so strong that it can affect your breathing. That would be really scary." A few minutes later she had a panic attack. By keeping a diary over the next couple weeks she discovered that she also had panic attacks after exercising and when lifting heavy objects. It soon became clear that strenuous exertion that caused her to be short of breath was one of the triggers for her panic.

The second goal is to then challenge the thoughts that led to panic. One should begin by admitting that many of the fears the person has may contain a grain of truth. Nevertheless, the feared consequences are very unlikely to materialize (e.g., there may be some chance of their being demoted, but is it a likelihood and would it really mean one's life was over?). The aim is to have the soldier at least intellectually acknowledge that these fears are not grounded in reality. This is simply a starting point for making further changes.

The third goal is to offer realistic alternative thoughts to replace the catastrophic fears the person normally entertains. For example, one might agree that not having passed the PT recently will be a bad mark on one's record, but it is not going to determine the course of his Army career. Nor will it bring great shame on him that can never be lived down. Could he be teased for failing to pass? Sure. Might someone in his chain of command give him a hard time? Absolutely. Is he likely to have to do remedial PT workouts? I suspect so. Will it make him an outcast, looked down upon with scorn by all, and demonstrate that he was never meant to be a soldier? Certainly not.

So, you go through this process and offer a reframe. The failed PT is likely to cause you some grief but nothing major nor lasting. It likely shows that you need to monitor your physical fitness level a little more closely than you've been doing. The good news is you are in control of that, and inasmuch as you have passed all your other PTs, there is no reason to think you will not pass the next one if you prepare.

This same approach is taken with each catastrophic idea that can be traced to the panic attacks. You then instruct the soldier to remind himself of these 'reframes' when next he begins to get anxious. It is important that he begins to challenge stressful thoughts as soon as he becomes aware of them rather than waiting for anxiety to build. It is much easier for reframing to lead to reassurance when anxiety is still low rather than wait until it has gained momentum and panic has begun to set in.

Some soldiers will, quite naturally, question whether they can talk themselves out of their anxiety. The answer, of course, is "No." It is, however, a good starting point. A way to slow down the thought processes that lead to panic. What's more, when practiced over time it will become a habit. Second nature. This is important because negative thinking breeds more negative thinking (and stress). Conversely positive thinking gives rise to more positive thinking, and the sense of well-being that accompanies a more optimistic perspective.

Exposure

This third leg of intervention is often the most difficult. It involves having the individual intentionally 'expose' himself to the situations that trigger panic attacks. The natural question to ask at this point is why would you want to do that? It is a matter of gaining mastery. Soldiers will understand the logic if you frame it in the same way that many military exercises are explained. These are designed to help prepare soldiers for combat, but done in such a way that allows soldiers to hone their skills prior to the actual engagement. In this manner, habits are developed that allow soldiers to respond automatically and more effectively when in a real combat situation.

Exposure to panic inducing situations should be carefully planned. It is a collaborative effort between you and the soldier. Develop a list of possible situations wherein panic attacks are likely to occur. Make a detailed summary including who else might be present; the fears that are likely to develop; possible responses other might have to the soldier; etc.

Then take the list of situations and rank them from most difficult to least difficult. Beginning with the least difficult situation,begin to rehearse with the soldier how he can effectively respond to fears that are likely to arise. You will want to emphasize the importance of having the soldier challenge his catastrophic thinking before it even begins to arise. Remind him (again) that by itself this will not keep him from feeling anxious, but it does help slow the process. In addition, remind the soldier to practice the relaxation techniques that you have already taught him. He should begin using these techniques at the very first sign of anxiety.

Having thoroughly rehearsed with you, the soldier is now ready to confront the real-world situation. He needs to pick a specific day and time that he will put all of his practice to the test. In some instances it will be difficult to make such a specific schedule. Do your best. When he returns to talk to you, after having gone through the exposure, carefully review how things went and provide encouragement.

Seldom do these exposures go exactly as planned, and it is not unusual for soldiers to report back that they ended up having another panic attack. The main thing in such a situation is to keep the soldier's motivation up for continued practice. Point out that this was not unexpected. It is not so much whether he had a panic attack but that he practices the skills and survived. Continued exposure will show him that with time the anxiety begins to lessen. When exposure to these low-level situations no longer produces panic, move on to the next higher stressful situation on the list you made and schedule exposures accordingly. Continue the progression until the situations at the top of the hierarchy have been mastered.

Summary of Chaplain Interventions
for Panic Attack Disorder

Relaxation Training.

Cognitive Restructuring.

Exposure.

RESPONSE TO
SEXUAL ASSAULT

*S*PC Alicia Chung loved her work. As a photo journalist with Combat Camera, she got to see more of the Army, and Afghanistan, than most other soldiers. One assignment might take her to the headquarters of a high-ranking officer. The next day she might be travelling with a convoy doing resupply missions to various COBs, and or getting a 'behind the scenes' look at the performance of a visiting country/western band playing for the troops.

Her favorite assignments, however, were with the infantry. She was too honest to pretend that foot patrols did not frighten her, but the adrenalin rush of going outside the wire and never knowing when she would come into contact with the enemy was addictive. She had been on numerous patrols and come under fire many times. Chung never failed to photograph these engagements, but she also never failed to pick up her M16 and return fire. It was this aggressive spirit, and an ability to easily fit in with battle hardened infantrymen, that caused her to be well liked among the troops.

SPC Chung had grown up in Seattle as an only child. Her parents, both of whom worked in the medical field, had high expectations for their daughter. She could not remember a time when she was not expected to achieve and excel. There were cello lessons, dance classes, science fairs and sports. "We don't expect you to be the best at everything sweetheart," her parents often said, "but we do expect that you will always do your best."

It was not until she was approaching adolescence that Alicia realized that her parents view of "doing your best" really did in fact mean "be the best" at everything you attempted. Some children would have been angry at the bind this put them in but not Alicia. She felt freed by her new-found insight. It was an impossible standard. Alicia could no more feel bad about not living up to this standard than she could feel frustrated by not waving her arms and flying. If it was impossible, why worry she reasoned.

It was that sort of well-balanced personality, coupled with an outgoing approach to life, that carried her through a remarkably calm adolescence and into college. She had chosen Gonzaga University because of its journalism program and the history of so many graduates later serving in the Peace Corp. Her plans were to become a photo journalist and travel the world.

There was only one major obstacle to fulfilling these ambitions. Her parents insisted that she pay half her college expenses. Nothing like having some 'skin in the game' to help a young person appreciate the college experience they reasoned. With this in mind, Alicia had joined the Army Reserves as a means to defray her expenses.

This pleased her parents immensely. Their daughter was showing responsibility and at the same time following in the footsteps of her grandfather who served in the 442ⁿᵈ Infantry during WWII. When enlisting, Alicia had made one stipulation: she wanted to be assigned to a unit involved in photojournalism. Fate, and a highly motivated recruiter, were on her side. A slot was open with the 982ⁿᵈ Combat Camera Company in East Point Georgia.

Alicia signed the papers in the recruiter's office and a few weeks later was headed off for basic training. The next phase of her Army career went smoothly as she transitioned into the 982nd and the rhythm of drill weekends.

Before long, her unit was called up for a tour in Iraq and she spent a year "in the sandbox" behind a camera. Alicia was in her element. Her assignments as a photographer, especially when sent out with infantry, filled her with excitement. Upon returning home Alicia immediately concluded "I have to get back, and the sooner the better."

When an opportunity availed itself the following spring to deploy to Afghanistan she jumped on it, and for perhaps the first time in her life flatly refused to give in to the demands of her parents (they had objected to her volunteering for that deployment, saying she had done her part and should wait to see if another deployment was even necessary).

Despite being crossed leveled into a different unit Alicia made friends quickly and found new opportunities to use her skills. She thoroughly enjoyed being deployed and found it difficult to imagine going back to college. She had found her niche. The structure, the camaraderie, sense of purpose, getting to do what she loved for a cause she deeply believed in gave her a deep sense of happiness.

Although her job caused her to frequently be away from base, Alicia was conscientious about getting to chapel whenever she could. Eventually, she began to attend some of the Bible studies led by Chaplain Reagan. He was immediately drawn to the young specialist whose infectious optimism reminded him of his own daughter. A warm friendship began to form.

Reagan was fascinated by the Chung's work, and in truth was rather envious of all she got to see and do. By comparison he thought himself to have a rather dull deployment. Although some chaplains frequently travelled to other bases his position did not allow it. At least not much. He felt confined, and slightly disappointed. So many of the soldiers who came to the chapel were engaged in work that took them outside the wire: going into villages where they would meet the locals; establishing new schools; etc. Even the veterinarian who attended chapel had more contact with the world outside the wire than did Chaplain Reagan.

The chaplain consoled himself by remembering that he was doing what he had been called to do. What's more, the close working relationship he had established with many of the soldiers was extremely fulfilling. Although he was not often able to go outside the wire, he could live vicariously by hearing SPC Chung's stories of her travels, and seeing the photos she kept on her computer.

It was when SPC Chung had not attended services for several weeks that Chaplain Reagan became concerned. He recalled in their last conversation that she mentioned an upcoming mission. Something about chronicling the lives of infantry soldiers. She had, as usual, been vague about the specifics of her assignment. Nevertheless, the chaplain knew that none of her missions kept her away from base for more than a few days.

Much to his relief she was once again at chapel the following Sunday. When they spoke after the service, however, there was a marked difference in her demeanor. The young woman, who in the past had always been smiling, outgoing and talkative, now appeared withdrawn, sad, and anxious. At first the chaplain thought little about it: he had seen it before in other soldiers. Problems on the home front, difficulties within a soldier's unit, or simply the grind of deployment: an infinite list of hardships and challenges that would alter anyone's mood.

Reagan knew that most soldiers found ways to adjust and before long snapped back to being their old selves. But this did not happen with SPC Chung. In the weeks that followed she remained quiet and pensive. When the chaplain would ask about her latest missions, or suggest that she might have some new photos to share, she just smiled politely and said she had to get back to her shop.

Others might have assumed that SPC Chung really was too busy, but the chaplain thought there was more. Something he could not quite put his finger on, but left him with an uneasy feeling in his gut.

With that in mind, Reagan decided to push things. The next Sunday, as soldiers were leaving the chapel, he spotted Chung and asked if she could spare a few minutes. She looked surprised but agreed to stay, taking a seat in one of the folding chairs and laying her M16 on the floor. After saying goodbye to those who had attended the service, the chaplain made his way across the room to where SPC Chung was sitting.

"Good to see you Alicia. We've not had a chance to talk in a long while. I was thinking maybe we could spend some time catching up on your latest adventures."

Looking uncomfortable she replied, "Maybe... But I can't stay long Chaplain... and I really don't have any new photos to show you. At least nothing worth sharing. Been kind of slow. Sorry."

Reagan reassured her, "I think you're being modest. Your photos are always interesting. But that's alright, maybe we could spend a few minutes catching up. Would that be OK?"

Without enthusiasm she agreed and they walked to his office which consisted of an oversized closet in the back of the chapel. The small room felt like a furnace. "Must be the fuse," Reagan said. "Give me just a second to reset this thing and I'll be with you." While fiddling with the cover to the window unit he quipped, "I think this is God's way of reminding me how unpleasant it would be to die an unrepentant sinner." The joke fell flat, as did most of the chaplain's attempts at humor. Whatever strengths he might possess, comedy was not one of them.

A moment later the unit roared to life sending a steady blast of Artic air into the small quarters. Chung was still standing and by this time looking a little confused. "Am I in trouble?"

Reagan was puzzled by the question. "Well, no, no of course not. Why would you be in trouble... least of all with me?" Chung visibly sighed with relief. "Um, well, I just thought... never mind. I'm just tired. Not thinking clearly." Reagan thought this reaction provided the perfect opportunity to be direct.

"SPC Chung, you're not in trouble, but I did want to ask how you are doing. I've noticed that you seem..." and here Reagan stumbled over his words. He didn't want to offend her, but at the same time he wanted to be clear about the changes he had seen. " You're different. In the past you came to chapel and were happy. You smiled, talked with others, joked around... you know? But over the past month or so you look like you have the weight of the world on your shoulders. A shadow of your old lively self. I hope I'm not being too forward in bringing this up, but if there is

something going on, some troubles back home... something on your mind... What I'm trying to say, without being too intrusive, if you're struggling in some way I would love to help you."

SPC Chung stared at Reagan for a moment without expression, then turned to look away. As silence filled the gap between them, Reagan decided to let it remain, to say nothing. After a while the young soldier turned back to the chaplain and began to respond. Her eyes were wet with tears. She began to speak but no words came out. In a softer tone Reagan continued, "Something is weighing on you Alicia. That's clear. I wish you would share it with me."

Chung continued to look at him, deliberating on how to respond. Reagan remained silent. He knew enough from countless times spent with distraught parishioners that there are moments when silence is the best tactic to encourage disclosure. Giving the her some space to decide if she wanted to confide what was on her mind seemed best.

Becoming more rigid as she sat on the edge of her chair she eventually answered. "I haven't told anyone. I haven't wanted to tell anyone," Chung said in a whisper. "Remember what I said to you about that mission with the infantry a couple months ago?" The chaplain nodded, "Did something happen on the mission? Was someone injured?" Without answering the young specialist continued.

"When we got back to base one of the officers asked me to debrief with him. I thought it would be a good way to get more information for the story we were working on so I said yes. As we were walking over to the TOC he asked if we could stop by his CHU to pick something up. He went inside and after a minute he opened the door and asked me to come in and wait. I know I shouldn't enter a male soldier's CHU but I was tired and it was hot and..." she began to drift off as though lost in the memory.

The chaplain felt a sudden surge of anger, tension, and dread. He knew where the story was leading. Tears were now rolling down her cheeks. As though the weight of her memories were too much to bear, the young soldier slowly slid from the chair and sat on the floor. With arms wrapped around her legs, she began to slowly rock back and forth.

In a soft voice she sobbed, "Why me, why me? I'm not even pretty."

Over the next hour the chaplain patiently listened, reassured, and asked just enough questions to know for certain what steps to take next. The story SPC Chung told was one of being raped in the 2nd LT's CHU, and afterwards being threatened that if she were to tell anyone the lieutenant would do everything in his power to embarrass her and end her career.

"I think this is what we call a classic case of he said, she said." the LT had said with a smirk. "Or should we say buyer's remorse? Either way, if you accuse me of anything I guaran-damn-tee that you can kiss your Army career goodbye. Who on God's green earth is ever going to trust themselves to be with a Combat Camera soldier who throws around accusations of rape? No one!"

Grinning broadly he concluded "No sweetheart, your career would be over… and honestly, the sex really wasn't that good. Something you need to work on."

She hurriedly stumbled out of the LT's CHU and in a daze staggered back to her own quarters, then showered and spent the rest of the night curled up in bed. Sleep would not come, and instead she spent the night reliving the rape and considering what to do. She had seen other women raise concerns about sexual harassment. Sometimes it was taken seriously, but there were many times when the accuser became a pariah, treated by her unit as though she were a leper.

By the time the sun rose the next morning SPC Chung had decided to bury the incident. To never mention a word to anyone and thoroughly blot it out of her memory. The problem, of course, was that this was impossible.

Memories of the rape plagued her throughout the day, and haunted her sleep each night. She was filled with a sense of fear. Shame and helplessness washed over her in waves that left her feeling disoriented. She did her best to carry on in the missions she was assigned, but her performance suffered. SPC Chung would later describe this time as one of living on the razor's edge of a mountain, where the slightest misstep might send her plummeting into a black chasm from which there was no escape.

Listening intently, Chaplain Reagan recognized the clear signs trauma. He reassured her that as painful as life was right now, with the proper help she would eventually feel better. In time healing could take place. Eventually she would find peace and clarity, and that the only one who should feel ashamed was the 2nd LT.

Although it took a great deal of persuasion, SPC Chung eventually agreed to go to the Sexual Assault Response Coordinator (SARC) on base and make an unrestricted report. From there she would go to Combat Stress Control. With regard to her career the chaplain reassured her, "I know the commander of the LT's unit. It's an odd coincidence, but he attends a men's Bible study that I lead. Let me tell you, I don't think for a second that he will put up with this... I can't offer any guarantees, but he seems like a squared away leader to me."

As it turned out the chaplain was correct. The commander took the accusation very seriously and fully cooperated with the Special Agents from the Army's Criminal Investigation Command (CID). The investigation was still ongoing when the 2nd LT finished his deployment. But three months after returning home he was brought up on charges of rape.

After a contentious trial he was found guilty and dishonorably discharged from the Army. SPC Chung also completed her deployment. In those remaining months Chaplain Reagan made a point of talking with her, providing support and doing what he could to help. It was a testimony to her strength that the bright young woman Reagan had come to know earlier in the deployment slowly started to emerge once more. There were bound to be many more challenges she would need to face in her return from this dark chapter of life, but the worst was now behind her.

Identifying and Responding to Sexual Assault

Sexual assault is all too common both in the civilian and civil sectors of our society. Obtaining data, however, regarding the exact frequency of such assaults is difficult. The reason for this difficulty is, in part, that the definition of sexual assault varies according to whatever researcher is conducting the study. Some will use a definition that only includes unwanted touching of breasts, buttocks and genitals, while other researchers use broader criteria that may include any unwanted physical contact. Still others define sexual assault as including instances when a woman has been the object of sexual remarks. Another difficulty with obtaining good statistics on the frequency of sexual assault is the hesitancy of individuals to report when they have been assaulted. This reluctance arises for many reasons including embarrassment, fear of reprisals by the aggressor, lack of faith that disclosure will result in punishing the perpetrator, and so forth.

With regard to the military *"The Department (DoD) uses the term "sexual assault" to refer to a range of crimes, including rape, sexual assault, nonconsensual sodomy, aggravated sexual contact, abusive sexual contact, and attempts to commit these offenses, as defined by the UCMJ"* (DEPARTMENT OF DEFENSE ANNUAL REPORT ON SEXUAL ASSAULT IN THE MILITARY, 2013, p. 62). It should be noted that the definition used by DoD has changed over the years as explained in the 2013 DoD Report on Sexual Assaultin the Military: "The definition of "sexual assault" in the UCMJ has changed several times over the last several years:

- For incidents that occurred prior to the changes made to the UCMJ on October 1, 2007, the term "sexual assault" referred to the crimes of rape, nonconsensual sodomy, indecent assault, and attempts to commit these acts.
- For incidents that occurred between October 1, 2007 and June 27, 2012, the term "sexual assault" referred to the crimes of rape, aggravated sexual assault, aggravated sexual contact, abusive sexual contact, wrongful sexual contact, nonconsensual sodomy, and attempts to commit these acts.

- For incidents that occur on or after June 28, 2012, the term "sexual assault" refers to the crimes of rape, sexual assault, aggravated sexual contact, abusive sexual contact, nonconsensual sodomy, and attempts to commit these acts" (p. 66).

Clearly, the definition of sexual assault has become broader, and in that sense captures a greater variety of behavior. On the other hand, with this broadening definition it has become more difficult to discern the exact nature of the behavior that is in question when reading a research report. For practical purposes, in the following discussion, sexual assault will refer to any unwanted physical sexual contact.

To be clear, not all unwanted sexual contact leads to a traumatic response. The soldier, for example, who is briefly kissed is much more likely to respond with anger and indignation than with trauma. Conversely, a soldier who is raped is likely to respond with a number of traumatic reactions. Although this common-sense distinction is sometimes missing from the psychological literature, it is best if we keep it in mind as we move forward in this chapter.

When an assault takes place it may be reported by one of two means. The first of these is an *unrestricted report* in which the data divulged is open for review by the commander and subsequently for criminal investigation. A *restricted report* may also be made, and this option preserves the service member's anonymity yet does not permit the criminal prosecution of the assailant, nor protect the service member from continued contact with the assailant (e.g., if they serve in the same unit they very likely will continue to work together in whatever capacity existed prior to the report alleging sexual assault). Using the 2012 definition of sexual assault described above shows that approximately 6% (26,000) of female military personnel were sexually assaulted in 2012 (DEPARTMENT OF DEFENSE ANNUAL REPORT ON SEXUAL ASSAULT IN THE MILITARY, 2013, p. 1). The 6% is derived from a projection using the number of service members who reported assault, and the number of service members who, from past research findings, are judged likely to have been assaulted but did not report.

Certainly this sort of methodological extrapolation has its faults, but given the consistency the DoD findings with similar surveys of the civilian population, the conclusions appear well-grounded. The take home message is that sexual assault (in a wide variety of forms) is a common and pernicious problem in the military. Although it is much more frequently seen with women, the evidence shows that nearly 1.5% of men also experience some form of sexual assault (DEPARTMENT OF DEFENSE ANNUAL REPORT ON SEXUAL ASSAULT IN THE MILITARY, 2013. p. 1).

The high incidence of sexual assault suggests that chaplains should be prepared to work with this population. Understanding the common emotional/behavioralreactions to sexual assault is essential.

One must keep in mind that assessing the *psychological* impact of sexual assault is often times similar to that of a physician examining a patient who has been in an automobile accident. There are common injuries associated with automobile accidents that a physician would want to be mindful of: contusions, fractures, lacerations, etc. But at the same time there are sufficient individual variations that it is impossible to list a specific set of injuries that will be found in all automobile accident victims.

The same holds true for the chaplain when assessing for the impact of sexual assault. There are some common reactions that most women experience, but there are a number of variations as well.

With this in mind what should the chaplain expect to find when talking to someone who has been sexually assaulted? The answer depends, in part, upon how recently the assault took place. If it was months or years ago the soldier may not show any signs of the trauma: they have either reconciled themselves to the event, or they have learned to control their reactions to the assault when in the company of others. If they do discuss the event you may find that they become agitated, tearful, momentarily seem lost in the memory of the event, or perhaps anxious. Some may dismiss the assault as unimportant because they have 'moved on' with their lives.

If the event is more recent then you are likely to find that the soldier becomes easily frustrated, is more withdrawn than usual, depressed, emotionally numb or feeling extremely anxious. As noted before, the responses to sexual assault are numerous and varied.

Course of Response to Sexual Assault

It is frequently the case that individuals who have been sexually assaulted are traumatized by what took place. Consequently, it is not uncommon for them to meet the diagnostic criteria for PTSD. Others who do not meet these criteria will nevertheless suffer from a variety of trauma symptoms (e.g., nightmares, hypervigilance, anxiety).

Over time these symptoms will often abate. For some the intense reactions that occur in the days and weeks after an assault slowly fade, but nevertheless remain ever present but at a lesser frequency. On the other hand, for those individuals who have a sturdy constitution, were free from significant mental health issues prior to the assault, and have a wealth of support from friends and families, it is not uncommon to find that they are able to re-assemble the pieces of their lives and resume living as they had prior to the assault. This is not to say that the assault was inconsequential. What happened will leave some tender points in their lives, but it does not interfere with their happiness, diminish the joy they receive from relationships, nor define their lives. The long-term course of recovery from sexual assault varies widely.

Assessment of Sexual Assault

Let's begin by assuming that you are not concerned to determine the veracity of the soldier's claim (for the sake of simplicity, in the following discussion we will simply assume that the disclosure is true). With this aspect of the evaluation put aside the question then becomes how does one conduct an assessment with a soldier who presents with allegations of having been sexually assaulted? The key in such assessments is to be reassuring, patient and persistent. Reassurance is important because the soldier is disclosing an event that very likely brings up emotions that are difficult to bear, and that they would very much like to avoid. Yet by disclosing these events to you most soldiers will find relief: they will have unburdened themselves of a secret, one that they likely find to be humiliating. Your reassurance helps relieve them of this burden, provide understanding and help them to find hope that life can return to normal.

Patience is demanded because the soldier is likely not to trust you (particularly if it is a female soldier and a male chaplain... but this should not dissuade you from working with the soldier). Be clear that you want to help, that you want to know what occurred but at the same time you understand that this is terribly difficult to discuss so you will proceed at their pace.

Persistence is necessary because many soldiers will waver in their desire to disclose what happened. They fear that they will be emotionally devastated by retelling, or reliving, the assault. They may also fear that you will not keep their confidence, or you may not believe them. By virtue of the reassurance and patience you demonstrate, however, these fears can usually be resolved. Even so, it often requires that you also persist in gently asking about the assault, making inquiries about the following:

When the assault occurred
How often the assault took place
How it unfolded
Who assaulted the soldier
What their relationship was prior to the assault
What has happened with the soldier since the time of the assault

Has the soldier ever been assaulted in the past (those with a
childhood history of sexual victimization are more likely to be
assaulted than those without such histories)

What impact has the assault had in regard to the following?

Emotional state (often fear, anger, depression and
a combination of these)

Functional responses (e.g., changes in appetite, changes in sleep,
changes in their desire to socialize, changes in attention/focus)

Changes in self-concept (it is common for victims of assault
to respond by feeling weak, vulnerable, dirty, foolish, etc.)

Changes in the soldier's sense of the future (e.g., does the future
now seem dreary and without hope)

Suicidality/self-harm (although not a typical reaction to sexual
assault, it should always be something that is examined).

Key Symptom Checklist for Sexual Assault

There are a wide variety of responses to sexual assault, but the
following are especially common.

Anxiety/panic attacks

Nightmares

Hypervigilance

Flashbacks

Depression

Avoidance of people, places, things that remind the soldier of
the assault

Hopelessness

General sense of betrayal

Stigmatization (e.g., feeling worthless, dirty, etc.)

Suicidality

It should be noted that when anxiety, hypervigilance, flashbacks, nightmares, and avoidance are all present as a cluster of symptoms, it is suggestive of PTSD.

Chaplain Interventions for Sexual Assault

The particular interventions one might employ depends majorly on the specific findings that come from your assessment. Generally, with sexual assault it is best if you can persuade the soldier to be seen by a mental health professional. Reminding them that therapists are also bound to keep confidential, the disclosures of soldiers may go a long way to making a successful referral. Moreover, it may be helpful to remind the soldier that receiving more immediate help from a mental health professional is likely to quicken the recovery process.

There will be times when the soldier still refuses to be seen by mental health, at least initially, in which case there is still much that you can do. If the responses of the soldier lead you to believe that PTSD is present then you should follow the protocol outlined in that section of this manual. Likewise if depression or anxiety are the main symptoms you should refer to those chapters in this manual.

In each case you will need to modify how exactly to respond to the specific concerns a soldier discloses. For instance, when someone presents with anxiety about being left alone, it would be counterproductive in the immediate aftermath of the assault to place great focus on the unrealistic basis of this fear. This will only convince the soldier that you do not understand.

A different approach is needed. You could simply sympathize with how difficult it must be to feel safe, and then move on to teach a variety of coping skills for dealing with the anxiety.

Lastly, many victims of sexual assault find it reassuring to learn that their reactions to the assault are common. That most people in their position have similar reactions, but with time and hard work these symptoms can be resolved. This offers hope that despite the tremendous distress currently experienced, there is every reason to believe that they will eventually reclaim their prior life, and indeed may end up stronger than before.

Summary of Chaplain Interventions for Sexual Assault

Refer to sections on PTSD, anxiety or depression as appropriate.
Provide reassurance and affirmation.
Instill hope in overcoming the current crisis.
Psycho-education regarding the typical responses to sexual assault.
Suicide assessment and preventative efforts as needed.

In addition, you will, with the soldier's permission, want to contact the Sexual Assault Response Coordinator (SARC) and/or Victim Advocate (VA) which are generally assigned at each brigade. Keep in mind as well Army Directive 2011-19 for *Expedited Transfers or Reassignment Procedures for Victims of Sexual Assault.* Very often soldiers who report sexual assault are then socially castigated by fellow soldiers in their unit, thereby undergoing further hardship and deepening their sense of shame.

The Victim Advocate can work in ways that enhance a commander's willingness to support the soldier. They may also be able to intervene with a commander if the perpetrator is part of the soldier's unit and attempts to shame her, or have her ostracized by her peers.

Although most commanders show compassion and support for those who have filed a sexual assault allegation, it is not always the case. Many feel torn between supporting the soldier who has made the allegation, and demonstrating good will toward the soldier who has been accused but not convicted. It takes wisdom, and mature leadership, to balance these concerns in a way that does justice to all concerned. When these qualities are absent the consequences can be tragic.

DRUG AND ALCOHOL ABUSE

I *t was early morning and icy ruts of dirt crunched under the chaplain's boots as he made his way to the DFAC. He walked with the natural gate of a plow horse and as he stepped around the deepest puddles of water his breath rose in puffs of grey condensation. "Don't recall the Army including this in their travel brochures for the Middle East." Brocker chuckled.*

The chaplain was on his first deployment to Afghanistan and although he knew the winters were cold, this information had largely been ignored in the pre-deployment training. Or, very possibly, he had slept through the Power Point presentation that covered this topic. With the endless number of pre-mob briefings, he really couldn't be faulted for taking a cat nap once in a while. At least that was what he told himself. Besides, the talk from fellow soldiers, those who had been on previous deployments, was always about the heat. "It's gonna be like living in a furnace" or, "Just about burned the skin off the back of my hands," was the common refrain.

Having forgotten to put on his gloves this morning, the chaplain slipped his hands into the pockets of his ACU trousers. Then, remembering Army regulations that forbid this small retreat to comfort, he decided it better to let his fingers freeze for the few minutes it would take him to get to the chow hall. Brocker grumbled "Half way around the world in a war zone and these are the things I need to worry about."

His mind drifted back to a time when he had just arrived on the base that would be his first duty station assignment. Standing outside the PX he absent mindedly paced back and forth while talking to a friend on his cell phone. Seemingly out of thin air a young LT2 briskly approached and reprimanded him for 'walking while talking on a cell phone.' It was at this point that Broker first realized he might have a tough time getting accustomed to Army regulations.

Despite the mild irritability he felt on this morning, the chaplain was generally an easy-going man and not prone to complaining. Cold weather, however, was his Kryptonite. When temperatures dropped to freezing, Broker became cranky. He blamed this tendency on having grown up in Hawaii.

The truth, however, was that Broker had a constitutional aversion to physical hardship. Whereas many of his military peers relished the experience of testing themselves against the elements, he thought it best to concede victory to nature and stay out of its way.

The chaplain enjoyed the creature comforts of life, and long ago he had made peace with whatever small misgivings this may have raised in others about his machismo. In light of these preferences, and the well-known demands that life in the military imposes, his friends at seminary were very much surprised when Broker informed them of his plans to join the Army. What no one knew was that the chaplain was equally surprised by his decision. Until the last year of seminary joining the armed services was a path he had never even considered. Not once.

This changed when he met Dr. Marshall, one of his New Testament professors. Dr. Marshall had served as a Navy chaplain in Vietnam, and when lecturing would sometimes illustrate a point by telling a story from his military days. These anecdotes of caring for Marines, punctuated with vivid descriptions of courage, heartache, and personal transformation, had deeply moved the young seminarian.

Over time the impact of these stories grew, and in turn a seed was planted that would push his career in an unexpected direction. Throughout the semester Broker would drop by Dr. Marshall's *office eager to discuss some theological question that required an immediate answer. Once there he invariably found a way to turn the conversation toward the topic of his professor's experiences living in a combat zone. A part of Broker felt likea voyeur because many of the stories Dr. Marshall told were of a personal nature. They seemed deeply intimate in the sense that even these many decades later the older man spoke with a moving concern for the young marines he had shepherded during those perilous months spent together.*

Broker could not help but notice how, when recounting some of these stories, Professor Marshall would occasionally pause, looking like a man who had been taken back in time. In other moments the older man would stop, his eyes misting briefly before he cleared his throat, then quickly pushed forward with his recollections. To be sure, however, not all of these stories were touched with heartache. Many involved events that caused both men to laugh heartily at the odd nature of men in a war zone.

As Broker's visits to his professor grew more frequent, so too did a picture of his life's mission. Like a photograph that begins as a blur of color and then slowly comes into focus revealing sharp lines, details and depth. During one of these conversation's the professor casually asked Broker if he had ever considered serving as a military chaplain. That question, expressed with an easy earnestness, pleased the young seminarian. The way in which his professor posed the question seemed to reflect that he clearly thought Broker could succeed within the military world.

It gave support to Broker's growing sense of direction, and affirmed within him that he could handle the challenges of working in a tough and demanding environment. Broker had not received much of this affirmation when growing up, and he basked in the professor's confidence like a teenage athlete who had been praised by his coach.

Throughout that semester Broker turned the question over in his mind like a jeweler inspecting a diamond. Was this the best path to take? Could he succeed in the military? Was it where God was leading? After much thought, discussion, and prayer, he decided that the chaplaincy was exactly where he needed to be. What's more, it was where he wanted to be... which was still true, even on a cold winter morning when headed to the DFAC.

After grabbing a breakfast tray and a large cup of tea the chaplain made his way into the main dining hall. It was still early enough that most of the long tables were empty. Over near the exit, however, he spotted a young warrant officer from his unit. "Morning Alex. Looks like you've decided to eat light today" Brocker quipped as he put down his tray. WO1 Alex Zebell was a very lean young man with a huge appetite. His breakfast was spread before him and took up a good deal of real estate on the table: there were pancakes, scrambled eggs, bacon, hash browns, a breakfast burrito, a bowl of cereal, and two glasses of juice.

" Yeah Chappy, I'm trying to lose some of those Christmas pounds I picked up recently going to all the fancy holiday parties around here. Got to keep up appearances when you're a role model for so many. Besides, I'm worried that my butt is getting too big."

*Typical Zebell, humorous, quick on the uptake, and **nearly always** self-effacing. The two of them had eaten many meals together, and the chaplain was always glad for Zebell's company. He was an agreeable young man with a lively mind and an abundance of enthusiasm. They spent some time talking about the weather, sports, then on to politics, and eventually a little conversation about work.*

About midway through the conversation, however, Brocker noticed that the young warrant officer was not quite himself. His eyes were somewhat bloodshot, and more obvious yet, his ability to concentrate seemed impaired.There was something on his mind... either that, or he was not getting enough sleep. Throughout their conversation Zebell seemed to drift off into his own thoughts. Eventually he finished nearly all of his breakfast, looked at his watch and said his goodbyes. Chaplain Brocker made a mental note to follow up with Zebell later in the week just to make sure he was taking care of himself.

More soldiers were filing into the DFAC now and the chaplain decided that he too needed to get moving. Remembering the cold walk he needed to make to get back to the chapel again regretted forgetting his gloves. "Going already Chaplain?" It was Chief Bray. Whereas Zebell was gregarious, funny and filled with enthusiasm, Chief Bray was his polar opposite: reclusive, serious as a heart attack with an undertaker's zest for life. Despite himself Chaplain Brocker cringed.

"Morning Chief. Yes, I was just heading over to the chapel."

"Well, we all have a job to do chaplain, and if you don't mind my taking a minute of your time, I would like to talk business."

"Sure Chief, what can I do for you?" the chaplain responded, reluctantly sitting back down at the table.

"Ummm, this may not be the ideal place to talk, but I don't know when I'll have time to drop by your office, so right now will have to do. But let's be discrete and grab an empty table." They made their way across the dining hall to a section that was still unoccupied, and after carefully arranging his breakfast tray, coffee cup and flatware, Chief Bray began to discuss his concerns.

"Saw you talking to Warrant Officer Zebell. I've got some concerns. Significant concerns. Before I confront him I wanted to get my ducks lined up."

"Sounds like you're going hunting Chief," the chaplain said with a smile.

Bray continued without sharing in the humor. "It's a serious matter, Chaplain. Zebell's work has been deteriorating. Steadily worsening over the last month or so. He's late coming into the shop, his assignments are seldom completed on time, his mind wanders, and he frequently forgets important information that has been relayed to him. I think, overall, he's a good soldier. But you wouldn't know that from his current performance." Bray paused for a moment and absent mindedly began to pick up two strips of bacon which he stuffed into his mouth.

"And you've spoken to him about these concerns?" Brocker asked.

"Of course I have," Bray shot back, sending small missiles of bacon flying across the table. "And at first this worked, you know. He straightened up for a short while. But not anymore. Sure, he says the right things, but his performance is in the crapper." Remembering with whom he was speaking the Chief's eyebrows shot up on his forehead looking like caterpillars squaring off for a fight. "No offense Chaplain. No offense."

"You've spoken to the commander already?" Brocker inquired.

"Not yet. I'd rather take care of it myself. But it's getting to the point that pretty soon I won't have a choice. That's why I'm talking with you. I've seen you two talking many times. Figure you know him about as well as anyone outside the shop. Maybe you can tell me what's going on with him."

"Wish I could help, but he hasn't told me anything that would make me think there's something wrong. And if he had confided in me, you know, in confidence that is, I wouldn't be able to tell you."

"Oh hell Chaplain, I'm not asking you to break your vows or whatever you call it. I'm just wanting to know if he's said anything. Something that would shed a little light on the situation. I'm not here to crucify him, I'm coming to you because I want to help him before the-- before everything hits the fan."

Chaplain Brocker paused for a moment. The Chief had a way with words. *"Sorry Chief, there really isn't anything I know about Zebell that would explain his faltering performance. He did seem tired this morning. Kind of zoned out, or worn out. You know, red eyes, distracted, just not himself. Looked like he had something on his mind, or then again maybe he just hasn't been getting much sleep."*

The Chief's eyebrows started vigorously dancing again when he heard this last comment. *"So you saw it too?"* he leaned in closer. *"Blood shot eyes, worn out and distracted. Well you can trust me when I say the man gets plenty of sleep. If the amount of time he spends holed up in his CHU is any indication, he's Rip Van F***ing Winkle. He may be worn out, but it's not because he's working too hard."*

Brocker was now more puzzled than ever. Before he had time to ask for an explanation Chief Bray stood up to leave. *"Thanks, Chaplain. That's helpful but I gotta go. Lots of work ahead. Think I'll just box this stuff up and take my breakfast to work. Hey, good talking with you."*

And with that he was gone. *"An odd start to the morning,"* Brocker thought, and made another mental note to check up on Zebell sooner rather than later in the week.

It turned out that the chaplain need not have made a mental note at all – the next evening, WO1 Zebell came to the chapel seeking his assistance. He described how he had left work early that day, telling the Chief that he was not feeling well. After spending a couple hours in his CHU there was a knock on the door. It was Chief Bray. He was accompanied by Staff Sergeant Frisker, and they had "dropped by" for a surprise barracks inspection. Zebell's stomach knotted as they entered the CHU. It took them little time to discover several empty cans of compressed air, three paper bags with nail polish remover inside, and a bottle of pain killers that had been prescribed to one Muriel Wheaton (Zebell's sister inlaw) for menstrual cramps. In addition, hidden under the bed were at least fifteen water bottles filled with urine.

When first confronted Zebell tried to explain away the incriminating findings. "This isn't what you think Chief. I work with computers all the time, you know that, and I can't stand to see them damaged by all this damn sand. Yeah, I go through a lot of cans of compressed air to keep things clean and operational."

The Chief was not in the mood to contemplate far-fetched excuses. "Sure you do, and then because you're such an environmentalist you take the empties back to your CHU for recycling. Right?" Barely taking a pause he went on. "And these bags with nail polish remover are probably used to get rid of the smudges all the female soldiers leave on keyboards when they disregard Army regulations and wear nail polish."

Bray was on a roll. He went on, his voice rising as he mockingly exclaimed that he had no idea why Zebell would have pain medications belonging to Muriel Wheaton, unless it was to treat the finger cramps he got from cleaning so many keyboards. Then, staring at the bottles of urine, the Chief began to say something but stopped himself.

"I'm taking all of this evidence with me. The meds, the empty cans, all of it. Start putting this crap in your duffel…Now!"

Zebell was so embarrassed and flustered he impulsively picked up a bottle of urine to put in his duffle. "Not those you idiot. All the other stuff. And once I leave, you've got 10 minutes to throw out your disgusting collection of piss bottles."

Zebell hurriedly put the incriminating evidence in his duffel and handed it to Frisker. He felt like a frightened juvenile delinquent. The chief quickly turned and slammed open the door of the CHU, barking over his shoulder, "Count on meeting with me tomorrow morning at 08:00 hours."

The staff sergeant had not said a word, but his expression was both stern and disappointed. Slowly, he too turned and walked out of the CHU, softly shutting the door behind him.

It took exactly seven minutes for Zebell to clean out what was under his bunk, and another five minutes for him to clean out the remaining recreational drug items that the Chief had not discovered during the inspection of his CHU. After sitting on the edge of his bunk for an hour trying to clear his thoughts the young warrant officer decided his best course of action was to speak with Chaplain Brocker.

After hearing the story, the chaplain leaned back in his chair. He liked Zebell, yet he could not help but think he might have let his affection for this young man color his opinion about the Chief's concerns when he first heard them the previous morning. At the time he had thought Bray was simply over reacting to the normal stressors that frequently impact the performance of many soldiers. But he had to admit the Chief was right. "Maybe I need to become a little more cynical," he thought to himself. Then, turning to the task at hand he asked Alex to tell him how long this had been going on, and what he wanted to do about solving the problem. Knowing the commander as he did, the chaplain thought there was a possibility that Alex could still finish his deployment. There would be a black mark on his record for certain, but less of a mark than being sent home early and possibly court martialed. If he were to avoid that fate, Alex would need to come clean about his drug abuse, and he would need to stop using drugs immediately. By the end of their conversation Chaplain Brocker was convinced that the young man was serious about turning things around.

"Listen Alex. I can't promise you anything about how this will all end up. What I can do is tell you that I'm happy to support you, but only if you make a real effort to clean this mess up. That means you put in a 110 percent effort. Any backsliding or screw ups means you're gone. You've

burnt all your bridges. There's no wiggle room for half-truths or trying to minimize what happened."

Alex had begun to feel a small flicker of relief learning the chaplain would support him. But hearing Brocker emphasize that there were no second chances felt like a gut punch. "What on earth have I gotten myself into?" he thought.

Chaplain Brocker put a hand on Zebell's shoulder. "Here's what we need to do. Let's head over to Combat Stress Control, see what they recommend for dealing with your drug issues, and where you might go for more help when we return home. After that we can talk about how to address Chief Bray when you meet with him tomorrow morning. If you want, I can go with you to that meeting… for moral support."

The meeting with CSC went well and the therapist with whom Alex met made several helpful suggestions. A plan was made to help him get traction in the initial stage of breaking free from his newly acquired drug habit. Likewise, a longer-term strategy began to take shape for providing more intensive help stateside.

Alone, heading back to his office, Chaplain Brocker reflected on the odds that Chief Bray would handle the matter by himself, or take it up the chain of command. Despite his faults, Bray was devoted to his men and had been known to put himself in the line of fire to protect them when needed. But when it came to drug abuse he felt it was likely the commander would be informed. "Either way," mused the chaplain, "If Zebell can get free of drugs, he has a chance to make a life for himself, even if it does not include being in the Army."

Identifying and Responding to Drug/Alcohol Abuse

The definition of alcohol or substance abuse (as well as the definition of dependence) varies according to the specific source one examines and how recently the resource has been updated. For our purposes we need not be too concerned about these differences. As a chaplain you do not need to make a definitive diagnosis regarding the abuse, or dependency upon, alcohol or drugs. Instead, the most important objective is to remain aware of when the soldiers use of drugs or alcohol has become problematic. Some general guidelines derived from (but not identical to) the Diagnostic and Statistical Manual used for making a psychiatric diagnosis of alcohol or substance abuse includes the following:

- The recurrent use of alcohol/drugs resulting in the soldier's failure to fulfill major obligations at work or home (e.g., repeated absences or poor work performance, suspensions, neglect of family responsibilities... all due or related to alcohol/drug use)
- Recurrent alcohol/drug use in situations wherein a reasonable person would conclude that this creates a dangerous situation (e.g., while operating heavy machinery; driving; prior to going to the firing range; prior to foot patrol; etc.)
- Recurrent legal problems related to use of alcohol/drugs (e.g., DUI, domestic violence charges while under the influence, disorderly conduct while under the influence, etc.)
- Service member continues to use alcohol/drugs despite the problems just reviewed that are caused or exacerbated by the effects of alcohol/drugs.

If within the past 12 months a soldier meets one or more of these criteria then it is very possible that he or she is struggling withdrug or alcohol abuse (perhaps both).

Unfortunately this is an all too common problem. Estimates of the incidence of alcohol and drug abuse generally suggest that over 20 million Americans deal with this problem. Within the military approximately 7% of active service members struggle with substance abuse (http://www.samhsa.gov/veterans-military-families).

As we look further at drug and alcohol issues it is worth noting that they occur along a spectrum of severity. When mental health professionals refer to abuse they generally are thinking of someone who meets the criteria just outlined. (As an aside, there is a growing trend to avoid using the term 'abuse' and replace it with 'harmful use' with the idea that it is less stigmatizing – this is a case of "A rose by any other name is still a rose").

A more severe form of drug and alcohol use is referred to as *dependence*. This occurs when the person has a physiologically based craving for these intoxicants, has developed some level of physical tolerance to their use (i.e., it takes more and more of the substance to create the same psychological impact), and likewise experiences physical symptoms of withdrawal when the substance is no longer available. If you are able to detect someone who is struggling with abuse you will almost certainly be able to detect those struggling with dependence. The symptoms of the latter are far more obvious and severe than those of the former. In either case, the best care for either abuse or dependency is to refer to a qualified mental health professional (one who specializes in the treatment of alcohol and substance addiction).

Course of Drug/Alcohol Abuse

The course of recovery from harmful drug or substance abuse varies depending on an individual's history of using these substances, the type of substance, educational level, race, sex, etc. When considering alcohol and drug treatments across the spectrum of services offered, the research suggest that between 40 to 60% of participants will eventually relapse.[12]. Moreover, only a little over 40% of those who enter such programs remain and complete the intervention. The good news, however, is that when individuals stay in treatment and receive the social support that is critical for such care the success rate is much

---

12 https://www.drugabuse.gov/publications/principles-drug-
    addiction-treatment-research-based-guide-third-edition/
    frequently-asked-questions/how-effective-drug-addiction-treatment

increased. It is also important to recognize that although relapse is common it is not a sign that the individual will never succeed in being free from addiction. Instead it is often simply one chapter in a long struggle toward achieving ongoing sobriety.

Assessment of Drug/Alcohol Abuse

When it comes to screening for drug and alcohol abuse there are two camps. One of these embraces the use of standardized questionnaires. They do so because a well-constructed questionnaire has been tested on hundreds (at times thousands) of subjects, and its ability to detect alcohol or drug abuse is well known due to the studies conducted during its construction.

The other camp places much more reliance on the counselor's interviewing ability, noting that questionnaires do not consider the non-verbal communication of a person answering questions, the capacity of a trusting relationship with an interviewer to elicit more information, nor the context within which some responses are made. Ideally, both these approaches could be used when the question of drug and alcohol abuse is being examined.

It is unrealistic, however, to expect a chaplain (or, for that matter, many therapists) to have the familiarity with issues related to addiction that would allow them to employ the sort of nuanced interviewing skills that an experienced addiction counselor possesses. Consequently, when you suspect that addiction or abuse may be an issue, it is best to rely most heavily on questionnaires.

But before you can hand out a questionnaire you need to recognize that it is needed. How do you get the soldier to candidly discuss his alcohol or drug use, thereby allowing you to know whether administering a questionnaire is needed? As with the interview process discussed with other disorders you will first focus on developing a sense of trust with the soldier. This is most likely to occur once you have patiently listened and empathized with him regarding the struggles that prompted him to seek you out. Only then do you move on to make more general inquiries about his life and background. A comment such as the following usually will suffice: "From all that you've told me I certainly understand why you feel the way you do. There is a tremendous amount of pressure on you right now and I'm glad you decided to talk with me. I would love to help. To be most helpful, however, it would be important for me to know a little more about you, that is, a little more about your background and also how your life is going in ways not related to what we've discussed so far. Mind if I ask you just a few questions?"

From that point you simply start with the least threatening questions and move on to those that may be more challenging. Where he grew up, how many children were in his family, what made him want to join the military, what does he do in his free time, does he have friends and what do they do together, etc.

Then to the more challenging questions, what sort of setbacks has he experienced in life? How did he respond (both the actual response and its impact on his confidence, outlook on life, etc.)? By the time you have reached this point in your discussion it will not at all appear unnatural for you to question whether he consumes alcohol?

It is a good idea to also remind the soldier that what he says to you is completely confidential. Stress this point. Inquire as to how often and how much he drinks. Does he do so only socially or by himself. Move on to whether he has ever used prescription or street drugs, perhaps when he was younger (placing it in the past makes answering less threatening). During the discussion you will want to determine whether there are unusual patterns of drug/alcohol consumption (e.g., in the morning, during work, etc.). Likewise, it is important to find out whether the soldier experiences diminished functioning when not using drugs/alcohol.

At some point while talking about the soldier's drug and alcohol use it will be helpful to normalize the use of these substances in order to reduce stress. To be clear, you are not condoning the use, but only noting that such 'self-medication' via alcohol or recreational drugs is common. This, in addition to reminders about confidentiality, will do much to advance candid responses.

If your discussion to this point has raised concerns about drug or alcohol abuse you will want to have the soldier complete one or both of the following questionnaires. Introduce them with the idea that you would like to get a little more specific information regarding this particular aspect of the soldier's life.

The first questionnaire is the Alcohol Use Disorders Identification Test (AUDIT). It is a 'screening' test. That is, a questionnaire designed to determine whether a problem with alcohol use exists. If a soldier's responses to the AUDIT are elevated (8 or more) then further evaluation by a mental health is recommended.

The second screener I want you to be aware of is the Drug Use Questionnaire (DAST). This comes in a longer form, 20 items, and shorter form with 10 items. The 20-item form is preferable as it is more comprehensive, but if the soldier is not likely to take the time to complete it then utilize the 10-item form. Cutoff scores are provided in the DAST that you will find within the appendix of this field manual. Instructions for its administration are straightforward and likewise found in the appendix.

There is one other avenue that a chaplain may wish to consider when assessing for drug and alcohol abuse. That is, if internet access is available have the soldier complete a more thorough questionnaire online.

Military Pathways offers just such an assessment tool and it can be found at http://screening.mentalhealthscreening.org/Military_ NDSD. Once at the webpage simply click on 'Take a Screening' and select from the menu.

Chaplain Key Symptom Checklist

Reliance on drugs/alcohol to reduce stress, anxiety, depression, etc.

Unusual patterns of drug/alcohol consumption (e.g., in the morning, during work, etc.).

Diminished functioning when not using drugs/alcohol.

Elevated scores on AUDIT or DAST.

Use online screening tools at

http://screening.mentalhealthscreening.org/Military_NDSD

Chaplain Interventions for Drug/Alcohol Abuse

When considering interventions it is important to keep one thing very clearly in mind: those who abuse alcohol or drugs arenot primarily addicted to specific substances, but rather to being intoxicated. This is not to deny that an addict has a *physiological craving* for whatever substance he prefers to use. What is more important is that he has a psychologically craving for the emotional effect these substances induce. A sense of wellbeing, a momentary escape from self-doubt, depression, anxiety, and loneliness.

This is worth keeping in mind. Physiological addiction occurs to specific drugs, psychological addiction is to intoxication. This is why it is of little value to think of a 'cocaine addict' as addicted simply to cocaine, or an alcoholic as simply addicted to alcohol. Each person has their preferred drug, but the goal of any drug when used to excess (including alcohol) is to escape psychological pain. It is the *impact* of the drug to which people have the strongest addiction, not simply a specific drug. This is why effective intervention must eventually address the underlying reasons for the addiction rather than focus simply on the particular drug(s) involved.

Although effective intervention is likely to require the soldier to enter into a formal drug and alcohol rehabilitation program, the chaplain can play an important role in helping the soldier along the road to recovery. To be of greatest help in this regard one must keep in mind that the person who struggles with an addiction is generally ashamed of themselves, expecting condemnation from others, and feeling hopeless about his future. Admittedly, this is not true of all individuals who have become addicted to drugs or alcohol, but it is certainly true for the vast majority. Particularly for those who have begun to feel the impact of addiction on their lives. What impact? The deterioration of family, loss of friendships, legal problems, careers that have been stymied or imploded, and much more.

With this in mind it is important that your posture toward the soldier with drug or alcohol related issues be one of empathy. This does not require you to approve of the addiction, far from it, but it does require that you attempt to understand what led the soldier to resort to drugs or alcohol as a solution to his struggles. By initially taking this approach you will win the soldier's trust and build a stronger alliance. Only by first establishing this type of relationship are you likely to persuade the soldier later on to seek more formal help through a drug and alcohol program.

Of course there will be obstacles along the way. Those who struggle with addiction tend to engage in a number of rationalizations in order to avoid confronting the extent of their problems. You should expect that the soldier will *minimize* the severity of their dependency on substances. They likely will also minimize the impact it has had on their lives. Others will simply *deny* altogether that it is a problem (the prognosis is somewhat worse in this case).

Alternatively, you will find some soldiers who blame others for the problem, deflecting their own responsibility. These justifications may take the form of "If only" statements. If only my wife would be more understanding. If only my commander would not make such unreasonable demands. If only I had received the promotion, and so forth.

In each case, whether it be minimizing, denial or deflection, your best response initially will be to explore the issue further with the soldier, rather than respond with a direct refutation. (Admittedly, direct confrontation is often used by drug and alcohol counselors, but the context of that counseling is different than that with which your work will take place. By the time a soldier is in a drug and alcohol rehabilitation program he has admitted that a problem exists, even if he has not been willing to fully accept responsibility. Consequently, counselors in these programs have a greater basis for responding with a direct confrontation).

By exploring the denial, minimization or blaming you are simply aiming to better understand one way in which the soldier views himself. This does not require you to accept any of these responses as valid, only that you show curiosity as to how their substance abuse is, from their perspective, not a problem (or at the least, not something for which they are responsible). Later, either in the same meeting or in a follow up meeting, you will press a little harder on these excuses. You can do so by pointing out the impact that the soldier's reliance on drugs or alcohol has created and expressing the opinion that this seems like a very serious consequence. Having the soldier begin to seriously entertain the idea that a problem exists is your goal.

Once this goal is reached, you will want to move onto psycho-education regarding addiction. This need not be a long discussion. There are just a few points to highlight in psycho-education. The first is that the soldier's reliance on drugs and alcohol is a symptom of a problem. Yes, it is a serious symptom, but the problem that gave rise to the abuse must eventually be dealt with in order to be successful. Most of the time the underlying problem centers on the distress caused by feelings of inadequacy, or guilt, anxiety and depression. These are concerns that the soldier has likely struggled with for some time. Eventually, he found that he could escape the distress, if only for a short while, by having a few beers, or taking some drugs. As his body adjusted to the alcohol and drugs he needed more in order to achieve the same sense of relief. That process continued to the point of addiction or abuse.

Often by the time addiction has occurred the individual finds that it is difficult to consume enough alcohol or drugs to experience the relief he seeks without also experiences the dramatic costs that come with it (e.g., drastically reduced job performance, loss of family and friends, DUIs, etc.). This dynamic is why the underlying causes that gave rise to alcohol or substance abuse must be dealt with eventually. But first it will be important to address the physical addiction. A two-step process. Emphasize that point.

The other point to get across in psycho-education is that the soldier is not the first person to have such a problem. Many examples may come to mind of public figures who likewise have struggled with addiction, and found a way to make a happy and successful life. This part of your discussion aims to relieve some of the stigma associatedwith drug and alcohol abuse. If you have examples of well-known people that have fought this battle your point will be made more forcefully.

As with other disorders mentioned earlier, developing healthy coping skills is an important task for the soldier who is struggling to overcome alcohol and drug addiction. As the soldier begins to refrain from using substances to cope with psychological pain, he will need alternatives. The coping skills mentioned earlier are easily learned. For some individuals they will provide enough relief to make the difference between immediately turning to alcohol/drugs versus getting through one more day sober.

Coping skills become even more powerful when combined with social support. Family and friends will be an important resource in this regard, but research shows that it is equally important for most individuals to align themselves with others who have firsthand experience struggling for sobriety.

Most military bases have AA meetings, and there are usually NA meetings that take place off base (although the military will often retain a soldier with alcohol related problems, it is extremely rare that they do so if it is a drug related problem, which is whyNA meetings are not found on military bases). Be sure to refer the addicted soldier to the type of meeting that best fits his or her needs. Most often it is possible to find AA and NA meetings taking place in different locations throughout the week. When first establishing sobriety, many soldiers will need to attend these meetings more than once a week.

There will be some individuals that benefit most by entering into an inpatient drug and alcohol rehabilitation program. The military has several such programs. Of course the soldier will be anxious that entry into such a program will either derail his career, or result in his receiving an 'Other Than Honorable' discharge (thereby losing a number of military benefits). Inasmuch as the military's response to substance abuse changes with time, it is important for you to remain current about current regulations regarding the impact that entry into a rehabilitation program will have on a soldier's career and benefits.

The successful outcome of your interview with a soldier that has abuse or dependency on drugs or alcohol is that he contacts the Army Substance Abuse Program (or the ADAPCP: Alcohol and Drug Abuse Prevention and Control Program). A referral to this program requires both the soldier's consent, and that the request go through the chain of command. Even so, it affords a wealth of assistance, and when entered into voluntarily the administrative consequences are often significantly lessened. By comparison, if the soldier continues to abuse drugs or alcohol the inevitable result will be dramatically impaired performance. In that case the chain of command will soon become involved in non-voluntary actions aimed at remediating the problem. The consequences in that instance are likely to be much more severe.

Summary of Chaplain Interventions for Drug/Alcohol Abuse

Support/understanding: most soldiers who struggle with alcohol and drug abuse feel isolated, frustrated, and insecure. They need someone who recognizes this sense of vulnerability while also seeing the potential for them to chart a different course in life.

Constructive Confrontation: most soldiers will initially object to any suggestion that they have a drug or alcohol related problem. Constructively confronting the soldier's denial, minimization, or tendency to blame others for their problems, while remaining supportive is essential for breaking down these barriers.

Education: it is important to provide some framework wherein the soldier understands how drugs and alcohol are often used to 'self-medicate' stress arising from personal problems. Information should also be provided about military programs available for the treatment of drug and alcohol related issues.

Coping Skills: introducing the soldier to alternatives for coping with stress can be very helpful. Those methods that work with one soldier may not work with another, so it is important to be ready to provide several different coping strategies for the soldier to try. Common methods include relaxation exercises, meditation, physical exercise, and social support. This last method is most important and best employed by involvement in AA or NA.

Referral to Army Substance Abuse Program (or the ADAPCP: Alcohol and Drug Abuse Prevention and Control Program).

TRAUMATIC BRAIN INJURY (TBI)

*J*oe Shackleford was an interesting soldier. He had been a standout college football player prior to joining the Army. Moreover, he had majored in mathematics and proven himself to be an exceptionally gifted student who in his free time enjoyed studying Boolean algebra. At 6'3" tall and weighing 250 pounds he was a walking contradiction to the "brawn without brains" stereotype applied to so many athletes.

Joe had just started his junior year of college when terrorists brought down the twin towers. By winter of that same year his dorm room was cluttered with application materials to various graduate schools and informational pamphlets from the Navy, Marines, Air Force and Army.

At 21 years of age Joe felt as though he were having a mid-life crisis. College football had been a lifelong dream, and his performance on the field had exceeded his wildest hopes. Indeed, he was – without question – one of the best outside linebackers in his conference, and it no longer seemed far-fetched to dream of being drafted into the NFL. More than one scout had approached both he and his coach. Although nothing was guaranteed, it looked promising.

Even if that career path went sideways there remained mathematics. When caught in one of his more reflective moments Joe would admit that math excited him even more than football. Nevertheless, he reasoned, a career in mathematics could wait... but pro football would not.

These were the calculations swirling through his mind prior to September 11, 2001. In the months following that dark day, however, Joe had a growing sense of unease. He felt that he needed to respond to the attack on America in a way that went beyond pasting flag decals on his truck and having animated conversations with his friends about the upcoming war. He struggled with the tension of wanting to simply pursue life along the same course he had always imagined, versus the growing compulsion he now felt to join the military.

By the end of football season these musings had led Joe to a conclusion: he would enlist in the Army at the end of the academic year.

Although military culture was new to Joe he adapted quickly. His years in football had taught him lessons that made the transition easier than it was for many of his peers: respect authority, remain focused, work as a team, always do your best, and use hardships as a means to grow stronger.

He had joined the service with one stipulation – he would be an infantryman. Given his mental gifts the recruiter urged him to take an MOS that would be more intellectually challenging. Joe refused. He was stubborn, he dug in his heels. Eventually the recruiter relented, and shortly after completing basic training, PVT Shackelford found himself attached to the 4th Infantry. A deployment to Iraq soon followed and by April 2003 Joe and his battle buddies were busy sorting out their gear as they settled into their new surroundings, an Army base near Tikrit.

The deployment passed quickly. By the spring of 2004 Shackelford and his unit were 'wheels up', headed back to the states. He felt relieved to be heading home, and proud of the work he had accomplished.

It didn't take long, however, for the 4th Infantry to be rotated down range again. By this time Joe had been promoted to the rank of Specialist. He felt proud to be on the promotional fast track, but the rest and reset phase back in the States had been far too short. It seemed they had no sooner gotten home before the train up phase began for their next deployment.

By the fall of 2005 Joe was back in Iraq, this time at a base not far from Baghdad. One evening, four weeks after their return to theater, Joe joined his squad on a Stryker mission. Thirty minutes after rolling out *of the gate the front right tire of his Stryker ran over a pressure plate that had been buried in the road not more than ten hours before. The force of the explosion lifted the 19-ton vehicle into the air before gravity caused it to reverse course and land on its side. Two of the infantrymen on board had serious injuries and were bleeding profusely. Two others were unconscious. Joe was one of these. All four men were medevac'd to a nearby CSH.*

By the time Joe was being rolled into the ER he had regained consciousness. One eye was dilated, and his head felt as though a team of offensive tackles had run over him. For the next two days he was kept at the CSH for observation. After that, seeming no worse for wear, the medical team approved his returning to the unit.

Joe was glad to get back, but his thoughts were focused on those buddies who had been taken to Landstuhl Army Hospital in Germany. "They're good, Joe," his Staff Sergeant had reassured him. "Stop worrying about them. When we get back stateside you'll see. We'll all go out for a beer and hear about the good times they've been having while we sweat it out finishing our tour. But until then you've got to get your head back in the game. No room for getting distracted." Joe knew he was right, and tried his best to refocus on the mission.

Life in his squad followed a familiar routine. There was the daily rhythm of briefings, followed by mission prep, leaving the wire, executing the plan, debriefings, chow, sleep, then waking up and pressing the 'REPEAT' button. Prior to the IED Joe had taken to all of this like a fish takes to water. It was his natural element.

Not any longer. His sleep was fitful and more days than not he was sluggish. "What the hell happened to my energy?" he wondered. "It feels like I'm an old man in his 40s."

When briefed about a mission he would forget key details and had to rely more and more on the copious notes he took to fill in these gaps. This worried him so much his stomach constantly knotted. An overlooked detail could compromise the success of a mission. Worse yet, much worse, it could put one of his brothers in jeopardy.

Joe's buddies also noticed a change. The once easy going professional had become irritable and short tempered. Try as he might to control it, Joe often lashed out at others for the slightest mistake or transgression. What his fellow soldiers did not know, however, is that he saved his worst criticisms for himself. Pretty quickly this led Joe to constantly second guess his own decisions. A profound sense of self-doubt began to take root.

The fatigue, lack of sleep, and growing social isolation took a heavy toll. But the headaches that pierced like a hot knife were the worst. These would come upon him suddenly, without warning, and made the task of concentrating nearly impossible. All of these challenges reinforced his growing sense that the war was making him an old man in a young man's body. The confidence that had been so much in evidence during the first deployment had evaporated.

Although he was still able to function, it took an extraordinary effort to do so at the level needed. He didn't want to complain, especially to his sergeants – that seemed like a sure-fire way to draw unwanted attention. Instead, almost on impulse, Joe decided to approach Chaplain McCleary one Sunday morning after chapel services. "Maybe just venting to someone will take the edge off" he reasoned.

With that in mind, as other soldiers walked out of the small chapel, Joe remained and loitered around the chapel card table where free Bibles, pamphlets, and small care packages were kept. Despite his best efforts to look nonchalant, it was obvious to the chaplain that Joe was waiting for something.

"Specialist Shackelford," the chaplain exclaimed with a smile, "You looking for something in particular?"

"Well, no. I mean, maybe. Looks like you have a lot of interesting material here," Joe said unconvincingly. Chaplain McCleary waited. "Maybe I'll just grab a Bible. I lost mine somewhere," Joe mumbled. Doubts about talking with the chaplain began to grow.

"Take whatever you like. Or, if you want, we can go and look at some of the books I have in the back of the chapel," McCleary offered. His initial impression was growing stronger: this young soldier had something on his mind. "Or then again," McCleary continued, "maybe you have some questions you would like to ask.... about church, the Bible, you know."

Joe hesitated. He didn't want to come across as weak. It wasn't in his nature to complain, and even less so to seem as though he needed someone else to solve his problems. But the chaplain seemed sincere, and he had heard good things about him from other soldiers.

McCleary, they said, was different. Joe had heard from one of his buddies that the chaplain started his career as an 11 Bravo, and even now sometimes went outside the wire with the ground pounders.

The command had opposed this when McCleary first announced his intentions. But the chaplain had the tenacity of a bulldog. "If I'm going to do my job effectively, I need to share some of the same hardships my men shoulder every day," he explained to the commander. Eventually McCleary was given the go ahead to "tag along at the rear" on a limited number of missions.

This 'tagging along', and his former life as an infantryman, had given the chaplain a measure of credibility he could not have otherwise earned, and ended up opening the door to many discussions with the young men in his care.

" Yeah, yeah, sure, I suppose I have some questions. If you have the time that is," Joe replied.

"Do I have time? Too easy. I set my own schedule, so yeah, I have time." Joe started to speak again when the chaplain broke in "It's almost 1230, and if we hustle we can still get to the DFAC before they close. Let's grab some chow and bring it back to my office."

McCleary was hungry, and besides, he figured the young Specialist was more likely to open up if they broke bread together. By the time they had gotten to the DFAC their small talk had covered sports, the weather, and home life. Joe was feeling like he had made a good decision. Back at the chaplain's small office, over the course of lunch, he began to talk about what was really on his mind – all that had happened since being hit with the IED.

Chaplain McCleary knew enough about the symptoms of TBI to be concerned. Many of the benchmark signs of the disorder were present: irritability, lack of sleep, change of personality, problems with focus, headaches, fatigue, and the like. But the chaplain also knew that Specialist Shackelford should be seen by the unit's doc in order for him to receive the specific help he clearly needed. After hearing what the chaplain had to say regarding TBIs Joe was relieved. It wasn't great news to think he might have a brain injury, but on the other hand, he could stop worrying that he was going crazy. Or becoming an old man. Things were finally starting to make sense.

They finished lunch, and as Joe began walking back to his unit, Chaplain McCleary made his way to Major Rucker's office to give the unit physician a brief description of the young soldier who would soon be coming to see him for a visit. "Sometimes," the chaplain thought to himself, "Being the guy who makes a good handoff is the best job in the world." He felt certain that Rucker would make the right call in getting Shackelford the help he needed.

Identifying and Responding to Traumatic Brain Injury

Traumatic Brain Injury (TBI) refers to an injury to the brain that typically is incurred by a sudden and violent force to the head. Although TBI is frequently referred to as the 'invisible wound' carried by many service members who deployed during the War on Terror, it can occur in any number of situations. These include automobile accidents, sports events, household falls, etc. TBI occurs along a spectrum of severity from mild to severe, and includes temporary impairment as well as permanent limitations.

The impact of TBI among troops is significant. It is estimated that approximately 15 to 23% of the US forces who served in Iraq or Afghanistan have suffered from mild TBI (Wojcik, Stein, Bagg, Humphrey & Orosco, 2010; Bell, Neal, Tigno, Roberts, Mossop et al., 2009).

Course of Traumatic Brain Injury

There is no one common course of progression from TBI that one can expect to track from the time of injury to maximum recovery. In large part this is due to the fact that the sign posts for recovery are predicated on what part of the brain has been injured. Rehabilitation, however, can help service members to regain some, or all, of the lost functioning they experience as a result of this injury. More severe injuries, however, are likely to be less responsive to such rehabilitative efforts. Even so, strategies can often be developed for minimizing the impact of the impairment even if no diminution of the injury itself is possible.

Assessment of Traumatic Brain Injury

To assess TBI the chaplain will want to determine whether the soldier has been in a situation that could have resulted in a head injury (even if no clear physical harm was incurred). This is most likely to be the case when working with soldiers in the Combat Arms. Questioning whether the soldier was in a vehicle hit by an IED, VBED, etc. is important. Was the soldier in an area receiving mortar fire and if so how close was he to the explosions? Was he in a vehicle that rolled over; does he engage in combative (where he may have taken an unusually hard fall); etc.

You will also want to pay special attention to the soldier's previous functioning. Were the symptoms present prior to the incident (the incident you believe may have caused a TBI)? If not, what was his functioning like at that time relative to the specific symptoms he now has? If the symptoms were already present have they worsened?

Although varied in its presentation, those who have suffered a TBI will generally have several of the following symptoms:

Common Symptoms Immediately After Injury

- Being Dazed, confused, or "seeing stars."
- Not remembering the injury.
- Losing consciousness (being knocked out).

Common Symptoms Later On

- Persistent headache or neck pain.
- Sensitivity to light and noise.
- Loss of balance.
- Changes in sleep patterns.
- Feeling tired all the time, lacking energy.
- Ringing in the ears.
- Loss of sense of smell and taste.
- Slowness in thinking, acting, speaking or reading.
- Symptoms that may appear to be mental health conditions.
  - o Sudden mood changes for little or no reason.
  - o Difficulty managing relationships.
  - o Chronic anxiety, depression, apathy.
- Short term memory loss.
- Getting lost or easily confused.
- Having more trouble than usual with.
  - o Paying attention or concentrating.
  - o Organizing daily tasks.
  - o Making decisions.

Key Symptom Checklist for Traumatic Brain Injury

History of head injury (or reasonable suspicion of head injury given history)

Symptoms (physical or mental) arise immediately after incurring the head injury

Onset of delayed symptoms (occurring days or weeks later) that
involve the following areas of functioning:

Cognitive Changes:

Memory

Attention

Ability to organize thoughts

More easily confused

Capacity to plan and execute tasks related to a plan

Changes in ability to speak and read

Physical changes:

headaches/neck pain

sensitivity to light or sound

loss of balance

changes in sleep

diminished energy

Mental health changes:

reduced capacity for maintaining relationships

depression/sadness

anxiety

apathy

Chaplain Interventions for Traumatic Brain Injury

In this regard your best approach will be three pronged.

One is psycho-educational as you explain why you believe the
soldier may be suffering from TBI.

Secondly you want to reassure the soldier that there is no stigma
attached to having suffered a TBI that it need not impede his career,
but that he will need to be examined up by a psychologist or physician in
order to make a definitive diagnosis and receive appropriate care.

Third, make a referral to whatever medical or mental health
professional you deem best under the circumstances. In a small
forward operating base this may be the Troop Medical Clinic, or

Battalion Aid Station. At larger facilities you may be able to choose between a Combat Stress Control clinic and a Combat Support Hospital (Level III hospital).

Summary of Chaplain Interventions for Traumatic Brain Injury

1. Psycho-education.
2. Reassurance.
3. Referral to a medical specialist.

PERSONALITY DISORDERS

*A*s Chaplain Kendle walked across the base toward the gym, he smiled and thought to himself, "At last, springtime. I thought it would never get here." The morning sun cast a golden light on redbud trees in full bloom, and a stretch of vibrant green lawn within the center of the parade grounds. After spending a year in Afghanistan the chaplain was grateful to be home.

It had been a difficult deployment: two months longer than planned, a high op tempo, and heartbreaking casualties. He was struggling to reacclimate, and felt certain that others in his unit, those who had been through much worse, were likely to also be having a hard time.

The mandatory re-deployment briefings he had attended back in Afghanistan included descriptions of what to expect upon returning home. With this in mind, he knew his reaction was not unusual. Even so, it felt confusing. Returning CONUS was a happy event. "So why do I always feel out of place? Like somethings about to go sideways?" He concluded there was nothing to do but take it a day at a time, get back into his normal routine, and things would surely sort themselves out. Part of that routine, this morning, was getting in a work out.

After checking in at the front desk of the gym he walked quickly to the treadmills. "Ah yes, my machine is open." He had his favorite treadmill and no one was using it. Major Kendle was a creature of habit. In his mid-40s he was single, never married, and had spent most of his time in the Army as a reservist. But after being called up for a second deployment he left his small church in Oregon to become a fulltime soldier. The decision was a difficult one, but he could not see any other solution – to remain would have placed an unfair hardship on the church as he continued to be deployed for a year at a time. There just wasn't any way he could stay when it took such a toll on his congregation.

After a brisk 30-minute run on the treadmill Chaplain Kendle quickly weaved his way around the growing number of soldiers who had begun to enter the gym and headed for the exit. As he was leaving, however, he heard a commotion at the front desk. Someone was upset, their voice loud and shrill. The man creating the spectacle was red faced and wagging his finger at an embarrassed looking female attendant standing behind the front counter. The crowd in the lobby had grown quiet as though they were an audience watching a theater in the round. With a final dramatic gesture the crimson man exclaimed "You can be sure that before you hear the bugles play retreat the base commander will have learned about this!" Turning sharply on his heels he stormed out of the gym.

Chaplain Kendle shook his head and smiled to himself. "So, the return from deployment didn't really do anything for Lieutenant Cushings mood... but his sense of theater seems to have grown even stronger." The angry man was 1LT Cushings and he had been with the 2nd Battalion, 1st Infantry Regiment out of Fort Lewis during their 2010 tour. Upon first joining the unit he had made a very favorable impression. He was likable, entertaining, confident, and had an easy-going charm that seemed that made others feel special.

Unfortunately, most people who got to know the lieutenant a little better eventually came to have a very low opinion of him. After a short time one came to see how quickly Cushing's reservoir of good will evaporated, revealing an ill-tempered and often self-centered individual.

The deployment was his first-time down range and during pre-mob he behaved as though he were a hardened war veteran whose principle role was to tell others how to do their job. His self-assurance was in no way encumbered by his lack of experience or expertise.

He was a young man who seemed to have unintentionally jumped on the fast track of remaining a junior officer. "That's a guy who is sprinting down the road and making absolutely no progress" was how one sergeant major described him. "Treadmill Cushings" had taken hold as a nick name, but one that was not shared in front of the lieutenant.

As he walked back to his quarters the chaplain's thoughts were focused on 1LT Cushings. He mused to himself that the Army has its share of quick-tempered soldiers. These can be tolerated, especially when they possess competence and put the mission first. Self-centered soldiers are a little less common, but with enough social graces they manage to get by. But self-centered, ill-tempered and socially arrested soldiers? The chaplain found it tough to see how that could result in any kind of happy ending in the Army.

By the time Kendle had gotten to the chapel later that morning, the incident had been forgotten. The day was off to fast start as he worked his way down the 'To Do' list that rested on his desk. Crossing off each item brought a small wave of satisfaction. It was just when the chaplain was pouring his fourth cup of coffee (and reminding himself once more that he needed to cut down on his caffeine intake) that he received a call from his commander, COL Smith. Apparently the young 2LT had not gone to the base commander after all but instead had gone to the Battalion Commander and made a complaint. Moreover, he had told COL Smith that Chaplain Kendle was in the gym and would testify to how poorly he had been treated by the front desk clerk.

"Candidly, Chaplain, I haven't got time for Cushing's tantrums. I'm not interested in whether the lieutenant got his feelings hurt by someone in the gym. What I am interested in is having this young officer get with the program, and if he can't then I will find a way to transfer him elsewhere... somewhere very far away from my command. I would like for you talk to him. You know, see if you can get him turned around. Lord knows I've tried to do that this morning with a little kick in the butt. Not sure it did any good, though."

Chaplain Kendle knew exactly what the commander meant. Cushings had proven such a disaster during their deployment that he had been relieved of his duties as XO. Nevertheless, he continued to cause problems in morale where ever he went and in whatever job he was assigned. Eventually the commander had put him in with the advance team to help with plans for their return CONUS.

That, too, had turned out poorly. His abrasive social interactions had so thoroughly irritated key individuals in Kuwait that they began to "lose" essential paperwork. This caused the unit to spend an extra week waiting for their flight home. Somehow other units continued to get a higher priority for securing flights back to the states. No one could be sure that this was payback for Cushing's bad manners, but then again no one would have mentioned it if it were true. By that time, however, Cushings had already returned home with the ADVON team and was not personally feeling the repercussions of his failed social skills.

"Not sure there is much I can do to help Colonel. He doesn't attend chapel, and he's seldom had much to say to me when we do have a conversation... which is infrequent." The chaplain stopped there and waited, hoping the Colonel would pick up the hint that there was nothing he could do to help out. When the Colonel did not respond and the silence began to drag on Chaplain Kendle realized a more straightforward approach was needed. "Really, would love to help, but given what I know about the guy I don't think he will listen to me."

The Colonel was in no mood to discuss the matter. "Roger that, Chaplain. Give me a call once you've had a chance to talk with the Lieutenant. No later than the end of the week. I want to nail this down quickly." The phone went dead. Chaplain Kendle sighed and reached for his legal pad. One more item for his to-do list.

Although the chaplain had planned on stopping by to talk to Cushings after work an opportunity availed itself earlier in the day. As Kendle was making his way through the chow line, he noticed 2LT Cushings sitting alone by one of the windows overlooking the greens. Ignoring the many empty tables around him Kendle walked over and put his tray *down opposite of the young lieutenant. "Mind if I break bread with you Lieutenant?"*

Cushings looked up from the Stars and Stripes he was reading and gave the chaplain a warm smile. "My pleasure Major. Please have a seat."

After a few minutes of small talk and sharing how good it felt to be home from their deployment Chaplain Kendle moved the conversation directly to the incident at the gym that morning. Despite being in a profession where tact and diplomacy were often important, he maintained the penchant of many small church pastors for being blunt. "I was at the gym this morning and couldn't help but overhear some of what happened at the front desk."

Cushing's looked annoyed at being reminded of the incident. "Oh, yes, seems like they need to step up the training they give to those people. I may have been a little too harsh in my reaction, but then again, I doubt that the woman who was hassling me will treat another soldier that way any time soon. So I guess I really provided something of a public service," he said with a laugh. "Can you believe it? Requiring me to show my military ID? Really? I'm a commissioned officer in the Army, just back from combat, and she's freakin telling me I need to show an ID. What does she think this uniform is? A Halloween outfit?"

Kendle thought the lieutenant would respond differently, maybe with a little embarrassment or an excuse for his over the top behavior. This response took him by surprise. "What would I need to do to show her I'm a soldier? Maybe come back from combat with a limb missing? Unbelievable," Cushings continued.

Kendle smiled to himself. True, they had gone on deployment, and they had both been through numerous mortar attacks on base, but he knew for a fact that Cushings had never gone outside the wire. Not once. In fact, several times he had been invited to go on convoys but invariably turned down the offers due to having "mission essential" work to complete. He appeared to be the one non-replaceable cog in the Army's war machine that could not be spared for even a moment.

"You said a combat deployment. I didn't know you saw combat, Lieutenant," Kendle responded, knowing full well that he had not.

Pushing his chair away from the table Cushings laughed. "Well, if you mean did I gear up with the grunts and get my mojo on to knock down doors or any of that crap, I guess not. But you and I were both in some pretty hairy situations chaplain. If that doesn't qualify as combat I'm not sure what does."

The chaplain was beginning to enjoy the conversation at this point. He was not at all interested in embarrassing the young man, but he found it fascinating that the lieutenant viewed his deployment so differently than most of the other soldiers in the unit. Whether they had been on numerous patrols, engaged the enemy in combat, or stayed on base to perform their duties, to a man they were rather matter of fact about their experience. Indeed, if anything they were reserved and humble. Frankly, that attitude was what the chaplain expected of a young lieutenant who had never been outside the wire, not to mention having been relieved of his duties.

"So, getting back to the thing that happened at the gym, that was all about you not having your military ID?"

"Damn straight," the Lieutenant responded hotly. "I mean of course we're all technically supposed to bring ID with us but give me a break. Don't I deserve a little more latitude than that after a deployment? Couldn't she give me a little respect?"

Kendle decided to push some. Maybe Cushings would begin to show a more balanced perspective if he could get beyond the "returning hero" veneer. "It's tough making the transition back. I think all of us are a little on edge. Maybe more than a little. And in some ways, you had it rougher than most – that is, with that change in your duties and all."

Cushings looked hurt for a moment, then his expression quickly changed to one of arrogance. "Oh, you've got it all wrong Chaplain. Once we got to theater the commander pretty quickly realized that I could do more than just be an XO. His plate was full, which was to be expected, so he needed someone who could act as his right-hand man if you know what

I mean. Fortunate for me, and I guess for everybody really, he saw me as the solution to his problem. Someone who could fill a number of the unit's needs. A guy who could grasp the big picture view of the mission and be counted on to fill in wherever a key player was required. It was a pain in the neck I'll admit, but I was glad to help out... even though it meant giving up my XO position."

Kendle made a concerted effort not to smile. Many in the unit, and all the soldiers working with command, knew that Cushings had been relieved of his duties. "Hmmm. I thought that the Command Sergeant Major was the Commander's right-hand man," the chaplain responded.

Cushings' retort was immediate, edged with thinly-veiled sarcasm "Sure, if you rely on chain of command flow charts. You and I both know that sort of "school house" knowledge doesn't get you very far when you're down range. And if running a unit our size was as simple as that, I suppose the Army wouldn't need officers like me or the Commander. But let me tell you something, and I'm speaking as someone who has a degree in organizational management: It's never that easy. Never. Simple example. If the commander could have gotten by in the usual ways why would he call on me to help head up the ADVON party? Why would he pull someone like me from theater to do that kind of work if all you needed to do was follow some Army Command flow chart? He had to think outside the box, break the so-called standard rules. That's how you make sure to get the mission accomplished. And I was glad to help. But I'll tell you this, I did think I would get some sort of recognition for my efforts. Call me crazy, but a Bronze Star wouldn't have been out of line for going that far above and beyond."

Cushings seemed to be talking to himself as much as to the chaplain at this point. Kendle had become quiet and seemed at a loss for words. Shaking his head as though he was trying to rid himself of a bad memory the lieutenant stood up and brought the conversation to a close.

"Listen, Chaplain, it's been good getting to sit down and share a meal with you. Just two veterans swapping war stories, right? Not that I mind

eating alone but I know many soldiers hate the idea of sitting by themselves in a chow hall. Bet you're one of them, am I right? Well, you have an open invitation to drop by my table anytime if you're wanting some good company and conversation with your meal. But I've got a million things to do so I better be shoving off."

With that Cushings turned and made his way out of the chow hall. Through the large window Kendle watched the figure of the lieutenant slowly receding. Looking down at his plate he realized he had hardly eaten. "The lieutenant's wrong, I really don't mind eating alone" he said quietly to himself.

Thinking about the conversation that had just ended Kendle concluded that there was little reason to expect Cushings would change his ways. Maybe later in life... but not now.

Everything the lieutenant had said was twisted around the belief that he was something special. From what the chaplain could tell this view of himself was impenetrable. How do you get through to a man who is so thoroughly committed to his own grandiosity?

The chaplain began to think about how he would summarize his observations for the commander. That Cushings had a strong and abrasive personality was a l r e a d y obvious. The thing that now came across more clearly was how impervious he was to different views that other people might have of his behavior. Then there was the issue of how highly he thought of himself. It went well beyond an overabundance of confidence. No, this was in another realm altogether.

As Kendle was leaving the chow hall and adjusting his cover it struck him: Cushings is a narcissist. He is the sort of person whose life revolves around his attempts to defend the idea that he is something special. And, of course, this includes lashing out at others who behave in ways that threaten his fragile narcissistic self-image.

"Well, I guess the Colonel was right" Kendle reflected. "There was something I could do to help sort all of this out after all. It's just not going to end the way I had hoped."

PERSONALITY DISORDERS

There are ten different personality disorders recognized in the most recently updated Diagnostic and Statistical Manual (DSM-V) of the American Psychiatric Association. It is beyond the scope of this field manual to explore the different diagnostic criteria, assessment strategies and intervention approaches for each of these disorders. Moreover, because helping someone with a personality disorder to make substantive changes is one of the most difficult challenges a therapist will face, it is not a topic that lends itself to short term pastoral care. It is, however, important that you realize that this category of mental disorder exists, and have at least a cursory understanding of how to identify personality disorders.

Personality disorders are fundamentally different from all the other disorders that have been discussed. The difference lies in the fact that personality disorders describe a dysfunction that stems from the way in which an individual's personality has developed. This may involve an orientation in which the person is extremely insecure and dependent upon others (Dependent Personality Disorder). Or it may be reflected by chronic hostility toward others, accompanied by a negative view of the world, and perpetual interpersonal conflicts accompanied by repetitively breaking rules (Antisocial Personality Disorder).

Perhaps you will come across a soldier who has an unusually inflated sense of self-importance, expects to be recognized for his outstanding achievements despite having little basis for holding this expectation, believes he is so special that only those who are particularly gifted can truly understand him, and tends to consistently exploit others (Narcissistic Personality Disorder).

Although other personality disorder typologies could be mentioned, these brief examples demonstrate the general idea of how this group of disorders involves a dysfunction that is integral and pervasive within an individual's personality.

Be aware, that any feature used in diagnosing someone with a personality disorder is also found in nearly everyone. Their specific qualities are not unique. What set the personality disordered individual apart are the pervasiveness, intensity, and rigidity of these qualities.

In some ways this is similar to the other disorders we have studied. The individual with clinical depression does not have specific qualities that are unique, but rather has qualities that are common to us all from time to time but which have become so pronounced that they momentarily overwhelm his life. So too with personality disorders, the difference being the disorder is generally not transient but lifelong.

Therapists who work with such individuals readily acknowledge that the counseling required to work effectively with these patients is extraordinarily difficult. Consequently the demands made on the chaplain are likely to be much greater when working with a soldier having a Personality Disorder than when working with someone who is depressed or anxious. This is not surprising. In the former case you are attempting to change a part of someone's personality, something central to how that person identifies him or herself.

In light of the difficulties associated with personality disorders, and the high level of training required for such work, it makes most sense for chaplains to take a somewhat simplified approach to helping these service members. That is, if you conclude that a soldier has a personality disorder you are well advised to refer to mental health services.

If the soldier is not amenable to that idea, you may still find that some relief can be had by using the same techniques discussed elsewhere in this field manual. That is, for the personality disordered soldier who is anxious you may wish to try to help bring some relief by using those strategies discussed under the 'anxiety' section of the field manual. Likewise for depression, adjustment disorder and so forth.

It is prudent, however, to recognize that the course of treatment in these instances, that is the path of progress in your working together, will be very different than were you to be counseling someone who did not have a Personality Disorder. It is inevitable that this should be the case because the reason for the soldier being depressed, or anxious, etc. are entangled in how that person views him or herself due to their particular personality.

For example, the Dependent Personality Disordered soldier may perpetually feel that you are not doing enough to help. These individuals have a perpetually unhealthy dependence on others. They expect to be let down (which they usually are because their expectations are unrealistic). You will be no exception. Eventually their expectations will be so high that no one could reasonably succeed in responding.

Another example would be the Narcissistic Personality soldier who believes himself to be so unique and gifted that no one can truly understand him. Here too you will eventually fail to be, in his eyes, perceptive enough to grasp the workings of his mind. He is likely to respond with disappointment and anger. No longer relying upon you for help is the most common way this ends.

In all these instances it is important to remain patient, gracious, interested and firmly recognize your limits. To do otherwise is to invite greater problems. For example, if a Dependent Personality Disordered soldier conveys the message that you have not done enough to be of help, and you respond by redoubling your efforts, the eventual outcome will be an exhausted chaplain. Perhaps exhausted and resentful (you are only human, right?).

In this example it would be important to recognize that the soldier's dependent personality style is likely to make him feel that no one does enough for him. In this case you might try and get the solider to recognize this pattern in his relationships, and find ways for him to fill the underlying need that is driving this perception (often, with dependent personality types, that need is for affirmation).

Making a herculean effort to help the soldier with a personality disorder can very quickly turn into a Sisyphean task that leads a chaplain to feel frustrated and filled with self-doubt. Do what you can within reasonable limits. Set appropriate boundaries for yourself in this regard.

When working with someone who has a personality disorder, it is easy to become overly involved. Clear boundaries regarding what you can do, and what you cannot do for the soldier, is the most effective way to keep from becoming embroiled in an unhealthy pastoral relationship with individuals who struggle with personality disorders. Pray for them, guide them, and console them, but keep clear boundaries all the while.

APPENDICES

ABOUT THE AUTHOR

Forrest Talley is a clinical psychologist with a private practice in Northern California. He completed his undergraduate work at the University of California, San Diego (UCSD), and earned a Ph.D. at Vanderbilt University. Clearly having a penchant for Deja vu experiences he then completed a clinical internship at UCSD, before returning to Vanderbilt for a two-year NIMH Post-Doctoral Fellowship focused on psychotherapy research.

Subsequent work included a brief time teaching in the university setting, private practice, over 20 years working at the University of California, Davis, Medical School, forensic work for the juvenile and family courts, lecturing nationally on the assessment and treatment of abused and neglected children, and nine years in the U.S. Army Reserves (with a deployment to Iraq in 2008/2009).

If you have questions, or suggestions for how this volume could be improved, please contact the author at info@forresttalley.com.

APPENDIX I

WHEN TO REFER
TO A MENTAL
HEALTH PROFESSIONAL

When a soldier speaks with you concerning a mental health concern, there will be times when you wonder if it may be best to refer him to mental health. How that question is answered is important. Refer too often and you may earn the reputation of 'that chaplain who is just going to send you to see a shrink." We want to avoid that outcome.

On the other hand, if you very seldom make a referral to mental health it could result in a large number of soldiers getting worse. Here too a negative reputation is likely to take root.

Making smart, appropriate referrals to mental health is essential. Fortunately, this process it is not difficult. You simply need to follow clear guidelines for making effective decisions.

The six considerations given below provide a roadmap for when to make these types of referrals.

ONE: Safety Risk

Does the soldier's anxiety, in light of his duties and responsibilities, impair his performance to such a degree that there is a risk of harm to himself or others? A soldier who works in finance may make mistakes due to anxiety that will result in delayed reimbursements. A soldier who operates a 50-caliber machine gun in the turret of an MRAP may be impaired by the same level of anxiety in such a way that the safety of his unit is put at risk. The higher the risk, the more likely it is that you should refer to mental health.

TWO: Responsiveness

Has the soldier's response to your efforts at helping been positive? That is, has he, or she, taken your advice seriously, tried to do what you have recommended, and has this resulted in some positive results? The more responsive the soldier, and the more he has seriously attempted the solutions you've offered, the less likely it is that you will need to refer to mental health unless his distress shows no sign of decreasing over time.

THREE: Number and Significance of Stressors

Are the stressors the soldier is facing major ones or relatively common and minor? Moreover, does the soldier relate a number of stressors or only one or two? The more significant the stressors, and the more numerous they are, the more likely it is that you will want to refer to mental health.

FOUR: Past Responses to Stress

Does the soldier have a history of being successful in dealing with life's difficulties, or is there a history of problematic responses to the challenges he has faced? In this regard look for a past reliance on alcohol, drugs, acting out, etc. in response to problems he has encountered in the past. When a soldier presents with a history of problematic or unsuccessful responses to stress then you should be more inclined to refer to the mental health team.

FIVE: Social Support

How much support does the soldier have both in his unit, among fellow soldiers on the base, and at home? When a soldier has a good network of support he is more likely to be able to respond to the stress he is encountering. Soldiers who have little support, and/or those who are hesitant to use the support that they do have, are more likely to need mental health services.

SIX: Nature and Permanency of Stressors

Are the reasons for the soldier's current distress transient and likely to resolve on their own in a short period of time, or are they more long lasting? If they are of a persistent nature (i.e., news that his wife has filed for divorce, a challenging commander, etc.) then referral to mental health services becomes more likely.

APPENDIX II

A BRIEF GUIDE ON HOW TO STRUCTURE A CLINICAL INTERVIEW

As a chaplain you frequently have soldiers seeking out your advice, reassurance and guidance. The majority of these interactions require you to be insightful, supportive, and capable of blending spiritual guidance with practical wisdom. There are times, however, when a soldier's disclosures will raise concerns. Something that he, or she, has said will cause you to suspect that a mental health issue may be present and needs to be addressed.

When this situation unfolds it will be beneficial if you feel confident in knowing how to move forward with a plan to explore the issue more thoroughly. Understanding how to get a soldier to open up to you about his or her oft times hidden thoughts and feelings is essential. A clinical interview accomplishes this task.

What follows is not meant to mirror how a psychotherapist would proceed in such a situation. Your job is not to emulate the approach of a therapist. There is no need to embrace that strategy.

The trust you have built with your soldiers, and the skills you have developed in the course of your career as a chaplain, are more than sufficient to carry the day. All that is needed is to have a *game* when faithfully executed, uncovers the information required in you to be of help to that specific soldier. The following guideline provides you with that plan.

Step One: The Warm Up

In this phase of the interview your main goal is to develop a sense of trust and rapport. Both of these qualities are vital in order that you be able to obtain complete and truthful responses to questions later in the interview. How you approach this step will vary depending upon the specific circumstances and individual with whom you are working. Nevertheless, in most instances you will want to do the following. You can remember the main components by using the acronym **F-FIRE** (Focus, Follow, Inquire, Reflect, and Empathize).

A. FOCUS: Put aside all distractions. This sounds obvious, yet I've seen it ignored even by therapists who should know better. Once you have concluded that the discussion you are in will become a clinical interview, you are faced with two choices: put aside all distractions and take the time to conduct an interview, or schedule another time to meet with the soldier when you will be able to give you full attention to the matter at hand.

B. FOLLOW: In the initial discussion follow the soldier's lead. If he, or she, is discussing family tensions and how being deployed has added to these stressors, show curiosity and some empathy. You do this even if you have information that leads you to believe the core problem is that this soldier has PTSD which is the primary reason for the current sense of being overwhelmed. There will be time to examine each of your questions later in the interview, but at first you must build bridges of trust.

C. INQUIRE: Periodically ask questions that require the soldier to disclose specific and somewhat personal information about his or her life. When a soldier discloses details of personal information, and it is received by you in an empathic and understanding manner, a stronger sense of connection is built. Using the last example of the soldier who complains of home front stress, you can easily ask for the name of the soldier's spouse and children, or inquire about how long the soldier has been married. These are small details but they often move discussions from the point of being somewhat abstract to very concrete and specific. In this way the individual with whom you are speaking is likely to feel more clearly known by you. Do not, however, ask so many questions that the flow of the conversation becomes halting or awkward.

D. REFLECT: Summarize and reflect on the information you have heard. A primary human need is to be understood. Often when a soldier is distressed he or she will also feel somewhat confused by the mixed feelings and thoughts that bear down on them. When a chaplain is able to bring some order and clarity to this experience, the soldier will feel both relieved and understood. Your job is not to provide Freudian like insight into the origins of the problem. Just aim to show that you are tracking what the individual in front of you has expressed. An example of this might be "I think I get what you are saying. You've been deployed for three months and most of your conversations with you wife involve her telling you about things that are going wrong at home, and it feels like she expects you to be able to fix these problems even though you are half way around the world. Does that sound about right?"

E. EMPATHIZE: Your goal is to gather information in order to develop an effective plan of action aimed at alleviating the soldier's distress. The more the man or woman sitting in front of you feels understood, and experiences a sense of connection with you, the more likely you are to receive accurate information. Someone who feels guarded discloses less information than does someone who feels that he/she can talk freely. With this in mind it is helpful to explicitly empathize with the soldier's distress when appropriate.

Short and simple statements will work well. Some examples include:

"That must be extremely difficult to constantly feel that way."

"If I had gone through something like that I imagine I might feel the same way."

"You've been carrying around a huge amount of stress not wanting to burden others. No wonder you have difficulty sleeping."

There is no need to go overboard. One or two honest empathic responses will adequately convey to the soldier that you appreciate the emotional cost of the struggle being waged.

Step Two: The Overview

In this phase of the interview you begin to look more closely at the presenting problem. Thus far you have followed the soldier's lead, but now it is time to make a shift in your approach and take control of the conversation. This is necessary in order that you make certain to have a clear overview of the presenting problem.

You want to begin to ask questions so as to learn:

When did the problem begin?

How does the problem impact the soldier's overall well-being?

How does the problem impact the soldier's performance?

What specific concerns does the soldier have with regard to this problem (that it will affect his/her career; its impact on family; how it reflects on his/her reputation, and so forth).

What attempts has the individual made to resolve the issue and did these efforts lead to any type of improvement?

Is there anyone that the soldier identifies (other than yourself) who might be of help in resolving the issue?

Invariably you will have other questions as well. It is best to keep this phase of the interview somewhat short (ten to fifteen minutes), which will require you to prioritize your questions and leave some unanswered for the time being.

Step Three: The Checklist

In this phase of the interview you will want to review the 'Symptom Checklist' you consider most relevant to the soldier's presenting problem. By this point you will have gathered enough information to have a tentative decision on the diagnosis that best fits with what you have learned. If there are a couple of diagnoses that appear possible then proceed by reviewing both checklists.

To help this step of the interview go smoothly it is advisable to have copies of the checklists (found in the appendices of this field manual) organized and easily available.

Step Four: The 'Check In' And Proposed Plan Of Action

In this final step you want to briefly summarize what you have been told, what you believe the problem to be, and propose a plan of action for resolving the problem. This step in the interview often turns out to be somewhat lengthy. It is well worth the effort to set aside a little extra time to carefully explain the reasoning behind your proposed plan.

By patiently responding to a soldier's concerns you increase the likelihood of forging an agreement on how to move forward. Once you have that agreement it is best to put the plan into action as soon as possible. If, for example, you have suggested that the soldier should speak with someone in mental health then the best course of action is to walk with the soldier to Combat Stress Control. Putting this off only encourages hesitation and makes it more likely that the plan will not be followed. If, on the other hand, you will be working with the soldier then it is a good idea to schedule the next appointment to occur within the next 48 hours.

One last thought on conducting a clinical interview. These consultations seldom go according to plan. Expect that things will go sideways. You will be interrupted despite your best efforts otherwise. You may forget one of the steps outlined above (not the end of the world). Some soldiers will remain guarded and refuse to cooperate despite asking for your help. It may even be that everything has gone exactly as planned and the soldier is re-assigned the next day to a new base.

This is the nature of things. Be prepared to improvise and adapt as the process unfolds. With experience you will grow more comfortable with these unexpected contingencies and learn to respond effectively.

APPENDIX III

KEY SYMPTOM CHECKLISTS

AND SUMMARIES

OF CHAPLAIN INTERVENTIONS

GENERALIZED ANXIETY DISORDER
(GAD)

(Pages 21 to 39)

Key Symptom Checklist For
Generalized Anxiety Disorder

Restlessness or feeling keyed up or on edge
Being easily fatigued
Difficulty concentrating or mind going blank
Irritability
Chronic tension
*Sleep disturbance (difficulties falling asleep, staying asleep, or restless
    and unsatisfying sleep*

Summary of Chaplain Interventions for
Generalized Anxiety Disorder

Psychoeducation

Providing a reality check about the soldier's fears

Disconnecting the habit of worrying from feeling safe (so the act of
    worrying does not provide a security blanket)

Teach relaxation skills

Identify triggers of anxiety

Recommend changes in soldier's lifestyle that increase will reduce
    anxiety

POST-TRAUMATIC STRESS DISORDER (PTSD)

(Pages 40 to 56)

Key Symptom Checklist for Post-Traumatic Stress Disorder

Re-experiencing the trauma
Avoidance of any reminders of trauma related experience
Hyperarousal (increased caution, hypervigilance, constant tension, irritability, mild paranoia)

Summary of Chaplain's Interventions for Post-Traumatic Stress Disorder

Referral to Combat Stress Control

Education about the military's policies regarding PTSD, the impact on career advancement, the support by others he is likely to find, etc.

Coordination with soldier's command when the individual's safety, or that of others is jeopardized. Confidentiality is to be maintained, however, per Rule 503 of the Military Rules of Evidence. This requires the chaplain to obtain explicit permission for such coordination. The service member may also benefit by having you act as his or her advocate. Examples of such advocacy include having the soldier remain deployed but in a different capacity, or conversely to be sent stateside for treatment. Your effectiveness as an advocate will often be enhanced if you are able to consult with professionals within the Combat Stress Control.

Educate the soldier on the symptoms and course of PTSD

Establish a point of contact with CONUS mental health professionals to assist soldier upon his return.

DEPRESSION

Pages (57 to 74)

Key Symptom Checklist for Depression

Depressed mood
Anhedonia (lack of interest in events/people/hobbies)
Lack of energy
Changes in appetite
Low self-esteem
Disturbed sleep
Diminished focus/concentration
Social withdrawal

Summary of Chaplain Interventions for Depression

Extend Empathic Understanding
Constructively Challenge Distortions
Schedule Positive Activities
Increase Social Activity
Promote Good Health Habits
Encourage: Gratitude
      Helping Others
      Prayer & Worship

THOUGHT DISORDERS/SCHIZOPHRENIA

Pages (75 to 85)

Key Symptom Checklist for Thought Disorders (With A Focus on Schizophrenia)

Hallucinations (may involve any of the senses: visual, auditory, tactile, olfactory)

Delusions (beliefs, usually of a personal nature, that have no basis in fact)

Odd behaviors (unpredictable agitation, bizarre posture)

Grossly disorganized thinking (often expressed through extreme difficulty completing tasks, including self-care)

Minimal speech or incoherent speech

Summary of Chaplain Interventions for Thought Disorders (With A Focus on Schizophrenia)

Psychiatric referral

Psycho-education & self-management of symptoms

Drug/alcohol referral as needed

Cognitive Behavior Therapy referral

Family support

ADJUSTMENT DISORDER

Pages (86 to 98)

Key Symptom Checklist for Adjustment Disorder

Symptoms that impair activities of daily living
Onset occurs within three months of a stressor
Symptoms are more severe than would be expected
No other mental health disorder (i.e., major depression, PTSD, etc.) is
  present

Summary of Chaplain Interventions
for Adjustment Disorder

Identify the stressor that precipitated the adjustment disorder, and any
  factors that are perpetuating the distress (especially look for
  unrealistic conclusions about the future, or about the soldier's
  self-worth: also look for the subsequent development of poor
  sleeping habits, overreliance on caffeine/nicotine, etc.)

In a supportive manner, confront the primary cognitive distortions
  associated with the stressful event and its aftermath.

Help keep the soldier involved in activities that provide constructive
  social interaction, and still other activities that provide a sense of
  enjoyment and are meaningful.

Consider referral for psychiatric consult if depression or anxiety are
  severe, or the disorder prevents the soldier from performing his
  duties as needed.

As always, remain aware of suicide potential and perform appropriate
  assessment.

SUICIDE ASSESSMENT AND PREVENTION

Pages (102 to 123)

Key Symptom Checklist For Suicide Risk

Is the soldier distressed (e.g., depressed, extreme guilt/embarrassment, hopelessness, anger, etc.)?

Have there been major disruptions in the soldier's life leading up to this distress (e.g., divorce, death of a loved one or close friend, demotion, loss of job opportunities, onset of major illness, etc.)?

Does the soldier express an intent, even if mixed with ambivalence, to end his life?

Does he have a plan, and if so is it a specific plan for ending his life?

Is the plan lethal?

Does the soldier have the means to carry out the plan?

Is the soldier unable to identify personally compelling reasons for not taking his life?

Is there a history of past suicide attempts?

Is there a history of impulsively acting out?

*The risk of suicide is greater as more of these questions are answered in the affirmative.

Summary Of Chaplain Interventions for Suicide Risk

Develop a 'No Harm' contract
Work to resolve the soldier's sense of guilt/shame or a
    sense that life lacks purpose
Teach practical problem-solving skills
Teach relaxation techniques (to reduce emotional dysregulation)
Frequent follow up contact until crisis is resolved, then taper
    accordingly

PANIC ATTACK DISORDER

Pages (124 to 143)

Key Symptom Checklist for Panic Attack Disorder

Accelerated heart rate/palpitations.
Profuse sweating not associated with physical exertion.
Trembling/shaking associated with anxiety.
Shortness of breath and/or sense of smothering not associated with
    physical exertion
Sense of choking.
Chest pain/discomfort associated with tension/anxiety.
Repeated periods of nausea unrelated to physical illness
Dizzy/lightheadedness
During periods of anxiety feeling as though 'things are not quite
real' Fear of losing control or 'going crazy'
Intense fear of dying without clear and present
threatNumbness or tingling in any part of the body
Anxiety accompanied by urge to flee or escape
Spending a great deal of time/energy worried about when a
    panicattack will occur
Avoiding people, places or situations in order to avoid anxiety

Summary of Chaplain Interventions for Panic Attack Disorder

Relaxation Training
Cognitive Restructuring
Exposure

RESPONSE TO SEXUAL ASSAULT

Pages (144 to 159)

Key Symptom Checklist for Sexual Assault

There are a wide variety of responses to sexual assault, but the
following are especially common.

Anxiety/panic attacks

Nightmares

Hypervigilance

Flashbacks

Depression

*Avoidance of people, places, things that remind the soldier of the
assault*

Hopelessness

General sense of betrayal

Stigmatization (e.g., feeling worthless, dirty, etc.)

Suicidality

***It should be noted that when anxiety, hypervigilance, flashbacks,
nightmares, and avoidance (of those things that trigger memories of
theassault) are present as a cluster of symptoms it is suggestive of PTSD.**

Summary of Chaplain Interventions for Sexual Assault

Refer to sections on PTSD, anxiety or depression as appropriate

Provide reassurance and affirmation

Instill hope in overcoming the current crisis

Psycho-education regarding the typical responses to sexual assault

Suicide assessment and preventative efforts as needed

With the soldier's permission, contact the Sexual Assault Response
Coordinator (SARC) and/or the Victim Advocate (VA).

DRUG AND ALCOHOL ABUSE

Pages (160 to 179)

Chaplain Key Symptom Checklist

Reliance on drugs/alcohol to reduce stress, anxiety, depression, etc.
Unusual patterns of drug/alcohol consumption (e.g., in the
*   morning, during work, etc.)*
Diminished functioning when not using drugs/alcohol.
Elevated scores on AUDIT or DAST
Use online screening tools at
*   http://screening.mentalhealthscreening.org/Military_NDSD*

Summary of Chaplain Interventions for Drug/Alcohol Abuse

Support/Understanding: Most soldiers who struggle with alcohol and drug abuse feel isolated, frustrated, and insecure. They need someone who recognizes this sense of vulnerability while also seeing the potential for them to chart a different course in life.

Constructive Confrontation: Many people who struggle with drug or alcohol abuse, when first approached, respond with denial. It can be helpful to constructively confront the soldier's minimization, or tendency to blame others for their problems.

Education: Providing information about how drugs and alcohol are used to 'self-medicate' the pain that arises from personal problems is important. Providing accurate guidance regarding the Army's response to drug and alcohol use/abuse is also critical in assisting the soldier to make informed treatment choices. At the time of this writing the Secretary of the Army had released a memo detailing significant changes in this regard (see Army Directive 2019-12 Policy for Voluntary

Alcohol Related Behavioral Healthcare). It is wise to remain current on changes in policy in order to accurately counsel a soldier. If uncertain, a consultation with a JAG officer is advised.

Help Build Better Tools To Keep In The Fight: Teach the soldier coping skills that can help reduce his/her reliance on alcohol and drugs for providing psychological relief. Common skills include: relaxation exercises, meditation, physical exercise, and social support. This last method is most important and best employed by involvement in AA or NA.

Referrals: Link the soldier with the Army Substance Abuse Program (or the ADAPCP: Alcohol and Drug Abuse Prevention and Control Program).

*Those methods that work with one soldier may not work with another, so it is important to be ready to provide several different coping strategies for the soldier to try.

TRAUMATIC BRAIN INJURY (TBI)

Pages (180 to 189)

Key Symptom Checklist for Traumatic Brain Injury

History of head injury (or reasonable suspicion of head injury given history)

Symptoms (physical or mental) arise immediately after incurring the head injury

Onset of delayed symptoms (occurring days or weeks later) may include:

> *Cognitive Changes:*
> > *Memory*
> > *Attention*
> > *Ability to organize thoughts*
> > *More easily confused*
> > *Difficulty planning and executing tasks*
> > *Changes in ability to speak and read*
>
> *Physical Changes:*
> > *Headaches/neck pain*
> > *Sensitivity to light or sound*
> > *Loss of balance*
> > *Ability to fall asleep or stay asleep*
> > *Diminished energy*
>
> *Mental Health Changes:*
> > *Reduced capacity for maintaining relationships*
> > *Depression/sadness/anxiety/apathy*

Summary of Chaplain Interventions for Traumatic Brain Injury

1. Psycho-education
2. Reassurance
3. Referral to a medical specialist

PERSONALITY DISORDERS

Pages (190 to 201)

Personality disorders are marked by rigid and unhealthy ways of thinking, and interacting with others. Unlike other mental health issues (e.g., depression or PTSD), the qualities that lead to a diagnosis of a personality disorder are an inherent part of the individual's constitution. They are thought to be at the core of their personality (which is why the label 'Personality Disorder' is applied).

There are a wide variety of personality disorders, making it impossible to effectively enumerate a list of symptoms and interventions applicable for this diagnostic category. It should be noted, however, that if you find a soldier is constantly in the middle of some drama, is perpetually taking advantage of others without any remorse, seems to delight in the suffering of his or her comrades, or is insufferably arrogant and easily offended, that soldier is likely to at least learn toward having a Personality Disorder.

It is generally accepted that helping someone who struggles with a Personality Disorder make significant changes in how they relate to others is extremely difficult. When successful these efforts typically take years of therapy. As such it is not possible to provide a short list of interventions specific to someone who has a Personality Disorder.

What you can do is treat the symptoms with which the soldier has presented (e.g., anxiety, depression, adjustment disorder, etc.), and encourage making contact with a mental health professional.

APPENDIX IV

THE BRIEF TRAUMATIC BRAIN INJURY SCREEN (BTBIS)

3 Question DVBIC TBI Screening Tool
Instruction Sheet

Purpose and Use of the DVBIC 3 Question TBI Screen

The purpose of this screen is to identify service members who may need further evaluation for mild traumatic brain injury (MTBI).

Tool Development

The 3 Question DVBIC TBI Screening Tool, also called The Brief Traumatic Brain Injury Screen (BTBIS), was validated in a small, initial study conducted with active duty service members who served in Iraq/Afghanistan between January 2004 and January 2005.

Who to Screen

Screen should be used with service members who were injured during combat operations, training missions or other activities.

Screening Instructions

Question 1: A checked [√] response to any item A through F verifies injury.

Question 2: A checked [√] response to A-E meets criteria for a positive (+) screen. Further interview is indicated. A positive response to F or G does not indicate a positive screen, but should be further evaluated in a clinical interview.

Question 3: Endorsement of any item A-H verifies current symptoms which may be related to an MTBI if the screening and interview process determines a MTBI occurred.

Significance of Positive Screen

A service member who endorses an injury [Question 1], as well as an alteration of consciousness [Question 2 A-E], should be further evaluated via clinical interview because he/she is more highly suspect for having sustained an MTBI or concussion. The MTBI screen alone does not provide diagnosis of MTBI. A clinical interview is required.

Question DVBIC TBI Screening Tool

1. Did you have any injury(ies) during your deployment from any of the following? (check all that apply):

A. Fragment

B. Bullet

C. Vehicular (any type of vehicle, including airplane)

D. Fall

E. Blast (Improvised Explosive Device, RPG, Land mine, Grenade, etc.)

F. Other specify: _____

2. Did any injury received while you were deployed result in any of the following? (check all that apply):

A. Being dazed, confused or "seeing stars"

B. Not remembering the injury

C. Losing consciousness (knocked out) for less than a minute

D. Losing consciousness for 1-20 minutes

E. Losing consciousness for longer than 20 minutes

F. Having any symptoms of concussion afterward (such as headache, dizziness, irritability, etc.)

G. Head Injury

H. None of the above

> **NOTE:** Endorsement of A-E meets criteria for positive TBI Screen

> **NOTE:** Confirm F and G through clinical interview

3. Are you currently experiencing any of the following problems that you think might be related to a possible head injury or concussion? (check all that apply):

A. Headaches

B. Dizziness

C. Memory problems

D. Balance problems

E. Ringing in the ears

F. Irritability

G. Sleep problems

H. Other
specify: _____

Schwab, K. A., Baker, G., Ivins, B., Sluss-Tiller, M., Lux, W., & Warden, D. (2006). The Brief Traumatic Brain Injury Screen (BTBIS): Investigating the validity of a self-report instrument for detecting traumatic brain injury (TBI) in troops returning from deployment in Afghanistan and Iraq. *Neurology, 66*(5)(Supp. 2), A235.

For more information contact:

Telephone: 1-800-870-9244

Email: info@DVBIC.org

Web: www.DVBIC.org

APPENDIX V

DRUG SCREENING QUESTIONNAIRE (DAST)

U sing drugs can affect your health and some medications you may take. Please help us provide you with the best medical care by answering the questions below.

methamphetamines (speed, crystal)	cocaine
cannabis (marijuana, pot)	narcotics (heroin, oxycodone, methadone, etc.)
inhalants (paint thinner, aerosol, glue)	hallucinogens (LSD, mushrooms)
tranquilizers (valium)	other

How often have you used these drugs?
☐ Monthly or less ☐ Weekly ☐ Daily or almost daily

	No	Yes
1. Have you used drugs other than those required for medical reasons?		

2. Do you abuse more than one drug at a time?	No	Yes
3. Are you unable to stop using drugs when you want to?	No	Yes
4. Have you ever had blackouts or flashbacks as a result of drug use?	No	Yes
5. Do you ever feel bad or guilty about your drug use?	No	Yes
6. Does your spouse (or parents) ever complain about your involvement with drugs?	No	Yes
7. Have you neglected your family because of your use of drugs?	No	Yes
8. Have you engaged in illegal activities in order to obtain drugs?	No	Yes
9. Have you ever experienced withdrawal symptoms (felt sick) when you stopped taking drugs?	No	Yes
10. Have you had medical problems as a result of your drug use (e.g. memory loss, hepatitis, convulsions, bleeding)?	No	Yes

Have you ever injected drugs?
☐ Never
☐ Yes, in the past 90 days
☐ Yes, more than 90 days ago

Have you ever been in treatment for substance abuse?
☐ Never
☐ Currently
☐ In the past

(For the health professional)

Scoring and interpreting the DAST:

"Yes" responses receive one point each and are added for a total score. The score correlates with a zone of use that can be circled on the bottom right corner of the page.

Score	Zone of use	Indicated action
0	**I – No risk** No risk of related health problems	None
1 - 2, plus the following criteria: No daily use of any substance; no weekly use of drugs other than cannabis; no injection drug use in the past 3 months; not currently in treatment.	**II – Risky** Risk of health problems related to drug use.	Offer brief education on the benefits of abstaining from drug use. Monitor at future visits.
1 - 2 (without meeting criteria)		Brief intervention

3 - 5	**III – Harmful** Risk of health problems related to drug use and a possible mild or moderate substance use disorder.	Brief intervention (offer options that include treatment)
6+	**IV – Severe** Risk of health problems related to drug use and a possible moderate or severe substance use disorder.	

ZONE OF USE CATEGORIES

I	II	III	IV
0	1-2	3-5	6+

Description of 'Indicated Action'

Brief education: Inform patients about low-risk consumption levelsand the risks of excessive alcohol use.

Brief intervention: Patient-centered discussion that employs Motivational Interviewing concepts to raise a patient's awareness of their substance use and enhances their motivation to change their use. Brief interventions are typically performed in 3-15 minutes, and should occur in the same session as the initial screening. Repeated sessions are more effective than a one-time intervention.

　　If a patient is ready to accept treatment, a referral is a proactive process that facilitates access to specialized care for individuals likely experiencing a substance use disorder. These patients are referred to alcohol and drug treatment experts for more definitive, in-depth assessment and, if warranted, treatment. However, treatment also includes prescribing medications for substance use disorder as part of the patient's normal primary care.

More resources: www.sbirtoregon.org

APPENDIX VI

ALCOHOL SCREENING
QUESTIONNAIRE (AUDIT)

Our clinic asks all patients about alcohol use at least once a year. Drinking alcohol can affect your health and some medications you may take. Please help us provide you with the best medical care by answering the questions below.

Patient name: _____

Date of birth: _____

One drink equals:

1. How often do you have a drink containing alcohol?	Never	Monthly or less	2 - 4 times a month	2 - 3 times a week	4 or more times a week
2. How many drinks containing alcohol do you have on a typical day when you are drinking?	0 - 2	3 or 4	5 or 6	7 - 9	10 or more
3. How often do you have four or more drinks on one occasion?	Never	Less than monthly	Monthly	Weekly	Daily or almost daily
4. How often during the last year have you found that you were not able to stop drinking once you had started?	Never	Less than monthly	Monthly	Weekly	Daily or almost daily
5. How often during the last year have you failed to do what was normally expected of you because of drinking?	Never	Less than monthly	Monthly	Weekly	Daily or almost daily
6. How often during the last year have you needed a first drink in the morning to get yourself going after a heavy drinking session?	Never	Less than monthly	Monthly	Weekly	Daily or almost daily

7. How often during the last year have you had a feeling of guilt or remorse after drinking?	Never	Less than monthly	Monthly	Weekly	Daily or almost daily
8. How often during the last year have you been unable to remember what happened the night before because of your drinking?	Never	Less than monthly	Monthly	Weekly	Daily or almost daily
9. Have you or someone else been injured because of your drinking?	No		Yes, but not in the last year		Yes, in the last year
10. Has a relative, friend, doctor, or other health care worker been concerned about your drinking or suggested you cut down?	No		Yes, but not in the last year		Yes, in the last year
	0	1	2	3	4

Have you ever been in treatment for an alcohol problem?
- ☐ Never
- ☐ Currently
- ☐ In the past

Zone/Level of Risk	I	II	III	IV
Men Total Score:	0-4	5-14	15-19	20+
Women Total Score:	0-3	4-12	13-19	20+

(For the health professional)

Scoring and interpreting the AUDIT:

Each answer receives a point ranging from 0 to 4. Points are added for a total score that correlates with a zone of use that can be circled on the bottom left corner of the page.

Score*	Suggested zone	Indicated action
0-3 : Women 0-4 : Men	**I – Low risk** (low risk of health problems related to alcohol use)	Brief education
4-12: Women 5-14: Men	**II - Risky** (increased risk of health problems related to alcohol use)	Brief intervention
13-19: Women 15-19: Men	**III - Harmful** (increased risk of health problems related to alcohol use and a possible mild or moderate alcohol use disorder)	Brief intervention or referral to specialized treatment
20+: Men 20+: Women	**IV - Severe** (increased risk of health problems related to alcohol use and a possible moderate or severe alcohol use disorder)	Referral to specialized treatment

Description of 'Indicated Action'

Brief education: An opportunity to educate patients about low-risk consumption levels and the risks of excessive alcohol use.

Brief intervention: Patient-centered discussion that employs Motivational Interviewing concepts to raise an individual's awareness of his/her substance use and enhancing his/her motivation towards behavioral change. Brief interventions are typically performed in 3-15 minutes, and should occur in the same session as the initial screening. Repeated sessions are more effective than a one-time intervention.

The recommended behavior change is to cut back to low-risk drinking levels unless there are other medical reasons to abstain (liver damage, pregnancy, medication contraindications, etc.).

Patients with numerous or serious negative consequences from their drinking, or patients with likely dependence who cannot or will not obtain conventional specialized treatment, should receive more numerous and intensive interventions with follow up. The recommended behavior change in this case is to either cut back to low-risk drinking levels or abstain from use.

Referral to specialized treatment: A proactive process that facilitates access to specialized care for individuals who have been assessed to have substance use dependence. These patients are referred to alcohol and drug treatment experts for more definitive, in-depth assessment and, if warranted, treatment. The recommended behavior change is to abstain from use and accept the referral. Referrals to treatment are delivered to the patient using the brief intervention model.

More resources: www.sbirtoregon.org

* Johnson J, Lee A, Vinson D, Seale P. "Use of AUDIT-Based Measures to Identify Unhealthy Alcohol Use and Alcohol

Dependence in Primary Care: A Validation Study." Alcohol Clin Exp Res, Vol 37, No S1, 2013: pp E253–E259

REFERENCES

Al-Huthail Y. R. (2008). Accuracy of referring psychiatric diagnosis. *International journal of health sciences*, 2(1), 35–38.

American Psychiatric Association. (2013). Diagnostic and statistical manual of mental disorders (5th ed.). https://doi.org/10.1176/appi.books.9780890425596 American Psychiatric Association (2013). Diagnosis and statistical manual of mental disorders, 5th edition. Arlington, VA: Author.

American Psychiatric Association, (202013). What Are Anxiety Disorders? Retrieved from https://www.psychiatry.org/patients-families/anxiety-disorders/what-are-anxiety-disorders https://www.psychiatry.org/patients-families/anxiety disorders/what-are-anxiety-disorders

Anxiety Depression Association of America (ADAA), 2019. Facts & Statistics. Retrieved from https://adaa.org/about-adaa/ press-room/facts-statistics

Ardito, R. B., & Rabellino, D. (2011). Therapeutic alliance and outcome of psychotherapy: historical excursus, measurements, and prospects for research. *Frontiers in Psychology*, 2, 270. Published 2011 Oct 18. doi:10.3389/fpsyg.2011.00270

Bartoszek, G., Hannan, S. M., Kamm, J., Pamp, B., & Maieritsch, K. P. (2017). Trauma-Related Pain, Reexperiencing Symptoms, and Treatment of Posttraumatic Stress Disorder: A Longitudinal

Study of Veterans. *Journal of Trauma Stress.* 30(3), 288-295. doi:10.1002/jts.22183

Barut, J. K, Dietrich, M. S., Zanoni, P. A., & Ridner, S. H. (2016). Sense of Belonging and Hope in the Lives of Persons with Schizophrenia. *Archives of Psychiatric Nursing*, 30(2), 178-184. doi:10.1016/j.apnu.2015.08.009

Beck, A.T. & Gellatly, R., (2016). Catastrophic Thinking: A Transdiagnostic Process Across Psychiatric Disorders. *Cognitive Therapy Research*, 40, 441–452 (2016). https://doi.org/10.1007/s10608-016-9763-3

Bell, R. S., Vo, A. H., Neal, C. J., Tigno, J, Roberts, R., Mossop, C., et al., (2009). Military traumatic brain and spinal column injury: a 5-year study of the impact blast and other military grade weaponry on the central nervous system. *Journal of Trauma.* 2009;66(4 suppl):S104–11. https://pubmed.ncbi.nlm.nih.gov/19359953/

Bolier, L., Haverman, M., & Westerhof, G. J. (2013). Positive psychology interventions: a meta-analysis of randomized controlled studies. *BMC Public Health*, 13, 119. https://doi.org/10.1186/1471-2458-13-119

Brady, K. T., Killeen, T. K., Brewerton, T. & Lucerini, S. (2002). Comorbidity of psychiatric disorders and posttraumatic stress disorder. *Journal of Clinical Psychiatry*, 61 (7), 22-32.

Bystritsky, A., Khalsa, S., Cameron, M., & Schiffman, J. (2013). Current diagnosis and treatment of anxiety disorders, pharmacy and therapeutics. *Journal of Pharmacy and Therapeutics*, 38(1), 30–38.

Cacioppo, J. T., Hughes, M. E., Waite, L. J., Hawkley LC, & Thisted, R. A. (2006). Loneliness as a specific risk factor for depressive symptoms: cross-sectional and longitudinal analyses. *Psychology of Aging.* 21(1), 140-151. doi:10.1037/0882-7974.21.1.140

Carta, M. G., Balestrieri, M., Murru, A., & Hardoy, M. C. (2009). Adjustment Disorder: epidemiology, diagnosis and treatment.

Clinical Practice and Epidemiology in Mental Health. 5, 15. ,doi:10.1186/1745-0179-5-15

Center for Disease Control, (2015). Emergency Department Visits Related to Schizophrenia Among Adults Aged 18–64: United States, 2009–2011. Retrieved from https://www.cdc.gov/nchs/products/databriefs/db215.htm

Cowan, D. N., Weber, N. S., Fisher, J. A., Bedno, S. A., & Niebuhr, D. W. (2011). Incidence of adult onset schizophrenic disorders in the US military: patterns by sex, race and age. *Schizophrenic Research*, 127(3), 235-240. doi:10.1016/j.schres.2010.12.005

Crocq,M.A.(2015).Histoire des traitements antipsychotiques à action prolongée dans la schizophrénie [A history of antipsychotic long-acting injections in the treatment of schizophrenia]. *Encephale,* 41(1), 84-92. doi:10.1016/j.encep.2014.12.002

Cronin, E., Brand, B. L., & Mattanah, J. F. (2014). The impact of the therapeutic alliance on treatment outcome in patients with dissociative disorders. *European Journal of Psycho-traumatology.* 5, 10. 3402/ejpt.v5.22676. doi:10.3402/ejpt.v5.22676

David, A. C. (2013). Cognitive Restructuring. Retrieved from https://onlinelibrary.wiley.com/doi/full/10.1002/9781118528563.wbcbt02

Department of Defense Annual Report On Sexual Assault In The Military, 2013
https://api.army.mil/e2/c/downloads/343174.pdf

Debra, S. (2019). What to Know About Hyperventilation: Causes and Treatments. Retrieved from https://www.healthline.com/health/hyperventilation

Fiske, A., Wetherell, J. L., & Gatz, M. (2009). Depression in older adults. *Annual Review on Clinical Psychology*, 5, 363-389. doi:10.1146/annurev.clinpsy.032408.153621

Forsyth, A., Deane, F. P., & Williams, P. (2015). A lifestyle intervention for primary care patients with depression and anxiety: A randomized controlled trial. *Psychiatry Research*, 230(2), 537-544. doi:10.1016/j.psychres.2015.10.001

Fredrickson, B. I. (2001) The role of positive emotions in positive psychology: The broaden-and-build theory of positiveemotions. *American Psychologist*, 56(3), 218–226. https://doi.org/10.1037/0003-066X.56.3.218

Friedman M.J. (2015) Strategies for Acute Stress Reactions and Acute Stress Disorder (ASD). In: Posttraumatic and Acute Stress Disorders. Springer, Cham. Retrieved from http://doi-org-443.webvpn.fjmu.edu.cn/10.1007/978-3-319-15066-6_6

Frueh, B. C., Grubaugh, A L., Yeager, D E. & Magruder, K. M. (2009). Delayed-onset post-traumatic stress disorder among war veterans in primary care clinics. *British Journal of Psychiatry*, 194(6), 515-520. doi:10.1192/bjp.bp.108.054700

Gadermann, A. M., Engel, C. C., Naifeh, J. A., Nock, M. K., Petukhova, M., Santiago, P. N., Wu, B., Zaslavsky, A. M., & Kessler, R. C. (2014). Prevalence of DSM-IV major depression among U.S. military personnel: Meta-analysis and simulation. *Military Medicine*, 177(8), 47–59.

Gejman, P. V., Sanders, A. R., & Duan, J. (2010). The role of genetics in the etiology of schizophrenia. *Psychiatric Clinics of North America*, 33(1), 35-66. doi:10.1016/j.psc.2009.12.003

Gorlin, E. I., Lee, J., & Otto, M. W. (2018). A topographical map approach to representing treatment efficacy: a focus on positive psychology interventions. *Cognitive Behaviour Therapy*, 47(1), 34-42. doi:10.1080/16506073.2017.1342173

Guo, X., Zhai, J., Liu, Z., Fang, M., Wang, B., Wang, C., Hu, B., Sun, X., Lv, L., Lu, Z., Ma, C., He, X., Guo, T., Xie, S., Wu, R., Xue, Z., Chen, J., Twamley, E. W., Jin, H., & Zhao, J. (2010). Effect of antipsychotic medication alone vs combined with psychosocial intervention on outcomes of early-stage schizophrenia: A randomized, 1-year study. *Archives of general psychiatry*, 67(9), 895–904. https://doi.org/10.1001/archgenpsychiatry.2010.105

Harvey, P. D. & Bellack, A. S. (2009). Toward a terminology for functional recovery in schizophrenia: Is functional remission a viable concept? Schizophrenia Bulletin, 35(2), 300-306. https://www.ncbi.nlm.nih.gov/pmc/articles/PMC2659311/

Hor, K., & Taylor, M. (2010). Suicide and schizophrenia: a systematic review of rates and risk factors. *Journal of Psychopharmacology*, 24(4), 81-90. doi:10.1177/1359786810385490

Institute of Medicine, (2014). Treatment for Posttraumatic Stress Disorder in Military and Veteran Populations: Final Assessment. *Military Medicine*, 179 (12), 1401.

Iribarren, J., Prolo, P., Neagos, N. & Chiappelli, F. (2005). Post-traumatic stress disorder: evidence-based research for the third millennium. *Evidence Based Complement and Alternative Medicine*, 2(4), 503-512. doi:10.1093/ecam/neh127

Jenkinson, C. E., Dickens, A. P., Jones, J. K., Thompson-Coon, R. S., Taylor, M., & Richards, S. H. (2013). Is volunteering a public health intervention? A systematic review and meta-analysis of the health and survival of volunteers. *BMC Public Health*, 13(1), 1-10, 10.1186/1471-2458-13-773

Kalin, Ned H., (2020) The Critical Relationship between Anxiety and Depression. American Journal of Psychiatry, 1, 365–367. https://doi.org/10.1176/appi.ajp.2020.20030305

Keithly, L. J., Samples, S. J., & Strupp, H. H. (1980). Patient motivation as a predictor of process and outcome in psychotherapy. *Psychotherapy and Psychosomatics,* 33(1-2), 87-97. doi:10.1159/000287417

Kessing, L. V. (2007). Epidemiology of subtypes of depression. *Acta Psychiatrica Scandinavica,* (433), 85-89. doi:10.1111/j.1600-0447.2007.00966.x

Lamers, F., van Oppen, P., & Comijs, H. C. (2011). Comorbidity patterns of anxiety and depressive disorders in a large cohort study: the Netherlands Study of Depression and Anxiety

(NESDA). *Journal of Clinical Psychiatry*, 72(3), 341-348. doi:10.4088/JCP.10m06176blu

Leeies, M., Pagura, J., Sareen, J. & Bolton, J. M. (2010). The use of alcohol and drugs to self-medicate symptoms of posttraumatic stress disorder. *Depress Anxiety*, 27(8), 731-736. doi:10.1002/ da.20677

Lisa, F. (2013). Suicide: What Therapists Need To Know. *American Psychology Associate*, 1-6. http://www.imhlk.com/wp-content/ uploads/2018/06/Suicide-What-Therapists-Need-to-Know. pdf

Liza, V., & Christina, D. (2011).Stress Management Techniques: evidence-based procedures that reduce stress and promote health, *Health Science Journal*, 5 (2), 74-89.

Manzoni, G.M., Pagnini, F., & Castelnuovo, G. (2008). Relaxation training for anxiety: a ten-years systematic review with meta-analysis. BMC Psychiatry 8, 41 (2008). https://doi. org/10.1186/1471-244X-8-41

Melinda S., Robert, S., & Jeanne, S. (2019). Therapy for Anxiety Disorders. Retrieved from https://www.helpguide.org/articles/ anxiety/therapy-for-anxiety-disorders.htm

McFarlane, W., Dixon, L., Lukens, A., & Downing, D. (2012). Recent developments in family psychoeducation as an evidence-based practice. *Journal of Marital & Family Therapy*, 38(1), 101-121. doi:10.1111/j.1752-0606.2011.00256.

McLean C. P., Asnaani, A., & Litz, B. T. (2011). Hofmann SG. Gender differences in anxiety disorders: prevalence, course of illness, comorbidity and burden of illness. *Journal of Psychiatry Research*, 45, 1027-1035

Morrison, G. S. (2009). Early childhood education today. Upper Saddle River, N.J.: Merrill/Pearson.

National Institute of Mental Health (NIH), 2020). Major Depression. Retrieved from (http://www.nimh.nih.gov/health/statistics/ prevalence/major-depression-among-adults.shtml).

National Institute of Mental Health, (2016). Opportunities and Challenges of Developing Information Technologies on Behavioral and Social Science Clinical Research. Retrieved from https://www.nimh.nih.gov/about/advisory-boards-and-groups/ namhc/reports/opportunities-and-challenges-of-developing-information-technologies-on-behavioral-and-social-science-clinical-research.shtml

National Institute of Mental Health, (2017a). Schizophrenia. Retrieved from https://www.nimh.nih.gov/health/topics/ schizophrenia/index.shtml

National Institutes of Mental Health, (2017b). Anxiety Disorders. Retrieved from https://www.nimh.nih.gov/health/topics/ anxiety-disorders/index.shtml

National Sleep Foundation, (2017). Sleep Hygiene. Retrieved from https://www.sleepfoundation.org/articles/sleep-hygiene

Ogrodniczuk, J., Taylor, S., Thordarson, D. S., Maxfield, L., Fedoroff, I. C., & Lovell, K. (2003). Comparative efficacy, speed, and adverse effects of three PTSD treatments: exposure therapy, EMDR, and relaxation training. *Journal of Consultant on Clinical Psychology*, 71(2), 330-338. doi:10.1037/0022-006x.71.2.330

Owen, M. J., Craddock, N., & O'Donovan, M. C. (2005). Schizophrenia: genes at last? *Trends Genetics*, 21(9), 518-525. doi:10.1016/j.tig.2005.06.011

Patel, K. R., Cherian, J., Gohil, K., & Atkinson, D. (2014). Schizophrenia: overview and treatment options. *P & T: A Peer-Reviewed Journal For Formulary Management*, 39(9), 638–645.

Patricia, K.(2015). DoD: Military suicide rate declining. Retrieved from http://www.militarytimes.com/story/ military/pentagon/2015/01/16/ defense-department-suicides-2013-report/21865977/

Perusini, J. N. (2015). Neurobehavioral perspectives on the distinction between fear and anxiety. *Learn Memory*. 22(9), 417-425. doi:10.1101/lm.039180.115

Rajji, T. K., Ismail, Z., & Mulsant, B. H. (2009). Age at onset and cognition in schizophrenia: meta-analysis. *British Journal of Psychiatry*, 195(4), 286-293. doi:10.1192/bjp.bp.108.060723

Sanderson, W. C., Arunagiri, V., Funk, A. P., Ginsburg, K. L., Krychiw, J. K., Limowski, A. R., Olesnycky, O. S., & Stout, Z. (2020). The Nature and Treatment of Pandemic-Related Psychological Distress. *Journal of Contemporary Psychotherapy*, 1–13. https://doi.org/10.1007/s10879-020-09463-7

Sansone, R. A., & Sansone, L. A., (2010). Gratitude and Well Being. *Archive of "Psychiatry (Edgmont)*, 7(11), 18–22.

Scotland-Coogan, D. & Davis, E. (2016). Relaxation Techniques for Trauma. *Journal of Evidence Information on Social Work,* 13(5), 434-441. doi:10.1080/23761407.2016.1166845

The Assessment and Management of Risk for Suicide Working Group, (2013). VA/DoD clinical practice guideline for assessment and management of patients at risk for suicide. Retrieved from http://www.healthquality.va.gov/guidelines/MH/srb/VADODCP_SuicideRisk_Full.pdf).

Timothy, J. L. (2019). What You Should Know About Suicide. Retrieved https://www.healthline.com/health/ suicide-and-suicidal-behavior

Thompson, B. L. & Waltz, J. (2009). Mindfulness and experiential avoidance as predictors of posttraumatic stress disorder avoidance symptom severity. Journal of Anxiety Disorders, 24, 409–415.

Tuerk, P. W., Yoder, M., Grubaugh, A., Myrick, H., Hamner, M. & Acierno, R. (2011). Prolonged exposure therapy for combat-related posttraumatic stress disorder: an examination of treatment effectiveness for veterans of the wars in Afghanistan and Iraq. *Journal of Anxiety Disorder*, 25(3), 397-403. doi:10.1016/j.janxdis.2010.11.002

Varvogli, L. & Darvir, C. (2011). Stress Management Techniques: evidence-based procedures that reduce stress and promote health, *Health Science Journal*, 5 (2), 74-89.

Velten, J.,, Lavallee KL, Scholten S, Meyer AH, Zhang XC, Schneider S, & Margraf J. (2014). Lifestyle choices and mental health: a representative population survey. *BMC Psychology*, 2(1), 58. doi: 10.1186/s40359-014-0055-y. eCollection 2014.

Verghese, A. (2008). Spirituality and mental health. *Indian Journal of Psychiatry*, 50(4), 233-237. doi:10.4103/0019-5545.44742

Wangelin, B. C. &and Tuerk, P. W. (2014). PTSD in active combat soldiers: to treat or not to treat. *Journal of Law Medical Ethics*, 42(2), 161-170. doi:10.1111/jlme.12132

Wojcik BE, Stein CR, Bagg K, Humphrey RJ, Orosco J. (2010). Traumatic brain injury hospitalizations of U.S. army soldiers deployed to Afghanistan and Iraq. *American Journal of Preventative Medicine*, 38(1 suppl), 108–16.

World Health Organization (2004). Promoting Mental Health. Retrieved from http://www.who.int/mental_health/evidence/en/promoting_mhh.pdf

World Health Organization, (2019). Suicide. Retrieved from https://www.who.int/news-room/fact-sheets/detail/suicide

Yaser, R. A. (2008). Accuracy of Referring Psychiatric Diagnosis. *Archive of "International Journal of Health Sciences (Qassim)*, 2(1), 35–38. PMCID: PMC3068718

Printed in Great Britain
by Amazon

78963131R00140